MONEY
LETTERS
2 MY DAUGHTER

Winner of the
2013 Book of the Year,
Adult's Money Management

EIFLE
Excellence in
Financial Literacy Education

A National Honor
Awarded by the
Institute for Financial Literacy

MONEY
LETTERS

2 MY DAUGHTER

JACKIE CUMMINGS KOSKI

This book was printed in the United States of America

Published by Money Letters, LLC

Second Edition

Connect with Money Letters online:

For bulk quantities of the book, speaking
engagements or other information, visit:
www.moneyletters2.com
or Scan QR Code with you Smartphone

CONTENTS

To Amber, my little angel; it's been a thrill to watch you grow into such a strong and beautiful person.

To my late father, James Cummings Sr.; thank you for giving me the high values and work ethic that have guided me throughout my life.

I love you both.

PREFACE

My dad raised six hardheaded kids in a small three-bedroom ranch home, in a small rural town, on a factory laborer's income. But he did it and never complained. He was proud and never asked anybody for anything. Sometimes I hated that because we had little or nothing of our own—no phone, no new clothes, and every Thursday before payday, an empty refrigerator. I truly don't know how he did it, but looking back, I so admire and respect how he lived and showed me how to live—with values, honesty, and pride, regardless of our place in life.

When I was a senior in high school, my dad was diagnosed with cancer, which took its toll in a matter of months. He died at the age of forty-nine. My dad never got to see me graduate from high school, go on to college, start my own family, or write this book.

I used to say that no one helped me with anything when I was paying my own way through college, but while writing this book, I realized, my father helped me the whole time. He helped me by teaching me how to stand on my own two feet and not expect anything from anybody. So I did, without pause, because that's just what I was taught.

Still, I despised the financial deficit we seemed to always be in growing up. I was too young to really understand why money was always so tight, but I vowed not to be in that same place after I became an adult and had my own children. I think that was a big part of the drive behind all the money decisions I've made—getting a college degree, paying off debts quickly, saving aggressively so I would always have something to fall back on, investing my money wisely, and striving just to be a proud member of the middle class.

After doing what I thought was a pretty good job of this (and still trying), I of course, wanted to pass my wisdom on to my daughter. Problem was, she didn't want to listen to anything I had to say once she hit fifteen.

Since she wouldn't listen to me, I decided to teach her all my life lessons and advice about money, *in writing*. Oh, and while doing that, I figured I would share what I had to say to her, with every man, woman, and child that was never taught the basics about money and personal finances, like me. Through my writings, I realized that this was my calling and the way in which I shall give back to society. My one-sentence soapbox is, *Most people know very little about money, and there is a desperate need for better financial literacy in the United States, starting with high school on through college and beyond.*

To stay true to myself, my daughter, and anyone else curious enough to take a moment to read what I have to say, I wrote this book with unyielding frankness. I gathered all my experience, knowledge, successes, and failures with money—coupled with more hours of research and study than it would take you to earn a four-year college degree—in order to give you *Money Letters 2 my Daughter.*

Acknowledgments

Thank you to my primary inspiration for this book, my favorite (and only) daughter, Amber. She gave me the ideas for most of the material in the book and challenged me as a parent every step of the way (in more ways than you know). She is my angel and motivates me to be a better person today than I was yesterday.

My other major inspiration is the most amazing man I know and my beloved partner, Howard Goldson. He always inspired me to think big and do great things. I am so grateful to have had you in my corner while writing this book, and it was your support and motivation that helped me to the finish line.

I want to thank the people that shared my childhood with me, who shaped who I am today—my family. You are much of the reason for my desire to write this book. Thank you to my mother, Mary Ellen Cummings, for being so proud of even my smallest accomplishments. To my closest sister, Gwen, who is often misunderstood, but let me be clear: I've always believed you to be smarter, stronger, and more courageous than me; you are my alter ego.

Thank you to my brother Charles, who helped me out at one of the most pivotal moments in my life—the college years. With no money and no place to call home, I will never forget that you let me share your place without asking for even a penny in return, and it helped me get through the tough four years of college and put me on my way. Thank you to my other siblings, James, Eleanor, and Marilyn.

Thank you to two of my closest "girls trip" friends, Supha Xayprasith Mays and Windy Nicholson, for their support—professionally and personally. We met as young girls in our twenties working at the home office of the huge conglomerate Walmart Stores Inc. in Bentonville, Arkansas. Just out of college and pursuing our respective careers, we formed a bond that we have shared with each other ever since, forgetting the fact that we have always lived hundreds of miles apart (and still do).

To my friend and the best saver I know, Jim Reed; thank you for your belief in thinking that I always know what I am doing when it comes to finances and making me feel smarter than I really am. To my good friend Durand Carroll, who always helped me "search my soul" to become a better person than I thought I could be. Also, to my hairstylist, friend, and owner of the Lady C Salon Spa, Caroline Hollingsworth; thank you for listening and always giving me your candid thoughts (hairdressers always give the best advice).

I greatly appreciate the people that I spent so much time with at *LexisNexis* in Dayton, Ohio, whom I not only call coworkers (former and present), but great friends who encouraged and supported me in maintaining the delicate balance of working in Corporate America while writing this book: Durand, Donna, Tobi, Tina, Phi-Van, Gisselle, Gloria, Larry, Lisa, Jeanne, Soren, Leslie, Angie, and so many others that gave me input for the book. I can't forget my wonderful field partners in New York and New Jersey: Josh, Veronica, Katie, Phil, Komal, Anna, Catherine, Jessica, Shobie, David, and Rupert.

My sincere thanks to a group of people who I consider to be way smarter than me, the members of the *BetterInvesting Cincinnati Model Investment Club*: Mary, Dene, Marge, Don, Marty, Mike,

Gerry, Craig, Larry, Kugi, Mark, Betsy, Michele, Frank, Ian, Cliff, and in memory of Rose Ramsey and Joyce Shinn. Thank you for being so genuinely willing to share your investing wisdom with me so that I could then share it with others. We've made some great gains on the investments in our portfolio, but the real payoff is how much we learned from each other. Now with this book, I want to pay it forward.

INTRODUCTION

*M*oney Letters 2 my Daughter is a series of letters from a mother to her daughter about all things dealing with money and personal finances. It's not about teaching you how to make more money, but how to better manage the money you have. It will inspire you to finally trade in your stress and anxiety about money, for knowledge and power.

Every letter starts with a lesson and ends with love. In between, is easy-to-understand advice and guidance about how to make the most of your hard-earned money.

Much of the book includes things that people have only learned *after* they've made life-changing mistakes. Only then do they ask the question, Why didn't anyone ever tell me that? Well, Mom is telling you now, along with hundreds of other people that are simply seeking some foundational knowledge about money.

Most people did not grow up with positive financial role models in their lives and were never adequately educated about money—not at home, not in school, and not even in college. So here is your "textbook" on money matters that will raise your financial IQ. The help that you will get in this book will give you the power to make better financial decisions.

Take a peek at the self-taught wisdom of this mother as she speaks to her daughter through her smart, no-nonsense *Money Letters*.

Mom's Pledge

I, Jackie Cummings Koski, being a sound mom and caregiver, promise to

Educate *before* giving advice

Offer support *before* judging

Acknowledge effort *before* failure

Provide facts *before* giving opinions

Teach the value of a dollar *before* giving money

Praise your accomplishments and *applaud* your choices

Be your *biggest* cheerleader for whatever game you choose

Give you the chance to rise on your own *before* picking you up

Guide you to the right road and allow *you* to choose the direction

Amber, I encourage you to make this same pledge to your own children as I watch over and laugh when I see you struggle the way that I did to try and be a good mom.

CHAPTER 1

Earning Money

Earning money is the first step and foundation for all your finances. Your standard of living and lifestyle will primarily be dictated by how much money you earn from your job and other sources. This starts the money management cycle.

Dear Amber,

You should know that one of the best ways to help you achieve your highest earning potential is by getting a college education. These days, a college degree is virtually a requirement in many professions. Without a college degree, you are likely to get paid less, be out of work more, and have limited choices.

If you look at the high unemployment rate in June of 2012 (about 8%), the unemployment rate of those without a college degree was far greater than those with a college degree. Almost three times as many college graduates had a job as opposed to those with less education. Just review the chart in this letter, and you'll see the difference education makes.

So those four years of learning and studying to earn a college degree will pay off for you for the rest of your working life. Well worth the invested time and money.

Unemployment Rate by Level of Education*

June 2012

12.6%   • Less than a high school diploma

8.4%   • High school graduates, no college

7.5%   • Some college or associate degree

4.1%   • Bachelor's degree and higher

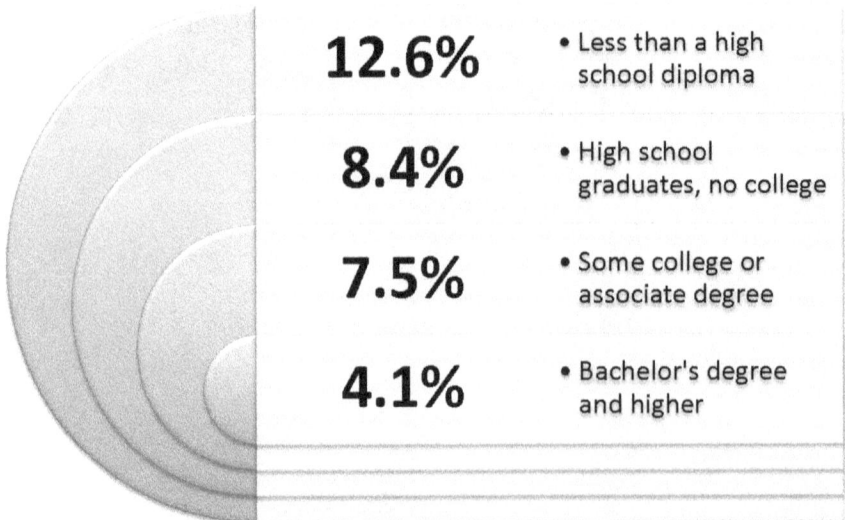

*Age 25 and older. Does not include active duty military or institutionalized individuals.
Source: Bureau of Labor Statistics, www.bls.gov

Should you be so inclined (or perhaps given an assignment in your economics class), you can find the latest unemployment stats broken down by just about every demographic you can think of at the US Bureau of Labor Statistics (www.bls.gov). Second thought, who am I kidding? You'll never do that, so just refer to my chart in this letter.

I highlight these unemployment numbers because many of your money decisions will depend on how much you earn. When you don't have a job, you don't have much money. If you don't have much money, it limits what you can buy, spend, save, and invest. It's all a chain reaction.

Love,
Pushing-the-college-degree Mom

*   *   *

Dear Amber,

When you begin your career and get your first job, you must negotiate your salary. The hiring manager at the company will often tell you that the salary is non-negotiable, but that is rarely true. Everything is negotiable. He or she just figures that coming right out of college, you don't know better and are not going to ask for more than you are offered.

Show them that you are smarter than the average job seeker, and do your homework so you know what that position should pay and why you might be worth even more (you graduated at the top of your class, you have drive and passion beyond your years, you have experience from an internship, you have a feisty mom that won't let you take any less than you are worth, etc.). Come to me and I will help coach you. You'll never get more than you ask for.

Love,
Stage Mom

*   *   *

Dear Amber,

As you navigate the working world and travel your career path, you'll learn a lot about getting the job you want. Over my working life, I think I have figured out the most important factors, which I have listed below in the order of importance:

1. Who you know
2. Timing
3. Luck
4. Education
5. Experience

You can almost always assume that the last two on the list—*experience and education*—will be characteristics of everyone in the running for the same job as you, so you might not have an advantage there. For the timing, if there is an opening, you and the other applicants are lucky that there is an opening for you to apply for in the first place. Even if you are lacking or otherwise not quite meeting the other four factors, who you know absolutely could get you the job over everyone else. So as you go through life, take careful consideration of all the people you meet, work with, interact with, and the friendships you make because they could very well be the connection you need to get your next job.

Love,
It's-who-you-know Mom

* * *

Dear Amber,

Working for Corporate America definitely has its benefits. But the thing you should try to always do is have some other income stream so that you have money from more than one source. It could be a hobby on the side like photographing weddings on the weekend or an investment property where you get rental income. By doing this, you are giving yourself a backup plan if something happens with your job, and in Corporate America, that could happen in a split second. Layoffs, downsizing, reorganizations, and other cutbacks within corporations happen all the time, and no matter how high up or how good you are, you could be given the boot.

Love,
Mom with a backup plan

*   *   *

Dear Amber,

As you go through college, you may, at some point, work in the service industry where you receive tips or will dine at restaurants where you will give tips. You'll hear all kinds of so-called guidelines, probably around 20%. That number is probably initiated by people in the industry, and the logic they use is that these poor servers are not paid enough by their employers, so you need to make up the difference. Well, my first job was at Shoney's in Aiken, South Carolina, as a server when I was in high school, making only $2.01 per hour plus tips. Even back then, I worked my butt off to make sure I got a good tip and never expected that someone had to tip me if I didn't give them good service.

After dining at hundreds of different restaurants in all categories, my best advice to you about tipping is this:

Every server must earn their tip. It is not a given or a requirement that you be the one to pay for their gap in salary. I start at a modest 15%, and it can go up or down from there. The ones that give good service get tips, as much at 20% to 30%, and the ones that give bad service are lucky to get 5%. It is up to the server how much they want to get paid. Exceptional service gets an exceptional tip; crappy service gets a crappy tip.

If you ever are asked to pre-pay a tip (like on a cruise ship), don't do it. How can you tip before you even know how good the service is?

Also, don't forget to tip a little something to service people like bellboys, hairstylist, hotel maids, and anyone else that you think went beyond their expected duty. These types of service people are often overlooked.

Love,
Carefully gratuitous Mom

*　　*　　*

Dear Amber,

Do what you Love, and you'll never have to work a day in your life. What the heck does that mean? you ask. Well, what that means is that you should find the thing in life that makes you the most happy, the thing that you are most passionate about, and the accomplishments that make you the most proud; and find a way to make money from it. That job may not even exist yet, but if you make it happen, it will not feel like work. Oprah Winfrey loved to talk, so she hosted a talk show for a living. Beyoncé loved to sing and dance, so she sang and danced for a living. Michael Jordan loved to play basketball, so he dunked for a living. They all loved what they did.

Love,
Mom with illusions of grandeur

*　　*　　*

Dear Amber,

I want to tell you about how to find money or property that may rightfully belong to you but somehow got lost in the system. Every state has an unclaimed property division, whose job is to hold money or property for persons within their state (past or present) that has not been claimed. Who would not want to claim money that belonged to them? Almost no one! But many times people may not realize the money is there for them. Anything from a forgotten deposit for your electric service to an insurance policy that you did not know you were the beneficiary of. Here are some of the most common types of unclaimed money and property:

- Bank accounts and safe deposit box contents
- Stocks, mutual funds, bonds, and dividends
- Uncashed checks and wages
- Insurance policies
- Utility deposits

To find out if there is any money a state has waiting for you, just go to www.missingmoney.com, a free website to search for unclaimed money and property. This site was established in 1999 and is officially endorsed by the National Association of Unclaimed Property Administrators (NAUPA), a nonprofit organization representing state governments. MissingMoney.com contains the official collective records from most state unclaimed property programs. Any state not included in the www.missingmoney.com database will have a link to that state's unclaimed property website.

Don't think that this is small potatoes because there are currently over $15 billion in unclaimed money and property being held by states seeking the rightful owners. Note that it is the states that hold and distribute this money or property, and they will never charge you a fee to do this (so stay away from shady characters that may try to charge you for this service).

The unclaimed property held by a state does not have a statute of limitations, so no matter how many years or generations have gone by, you still have the right to collect money held for you by the state.

State unclaimed property divisions do make active efforts to locate the individuals that the money or property rightfully belongs to. So I must say that this is a noble effort of the government on behalf of its citizens.

Love,
Mom believing that every dollar has an owner

*   *   *

Dear Amber,

Even though I know you will try very hard to earn your living by having a job and bringing home a paycheck, there may come a time when things get tough. You may lose your job or experience other kinds of temporary setbacks. Of course, this is the main reason for having an emergency fund, but I also want you to know that there is some government assistance that may be available to help you as well.

In 2012, the US government offered over six hundred programs spread across all fifty states and the District of Columbia. You can go to the government benefits website at www.benefits.gov and search by state, category, or agency. There are programs that provide assistance in the areas of unemployment, food, energy/utilities, healthcare, education, child care, housing, and many others.

The programs are meant to be *temporary*, so use them to help you transition to getting back on your feet as quickly as possible. And believe me, there will be many other people that you will be clearing the way for, that are falling on harder times than you, and are in need of the assistance much more than you.

Love,
Mom reluctantly supporting temporary assistance

*   *   *

CHAPTER 2

Spending Money

Spending money is something that I know you need very little instruction on. Many people get into financial trouble because of overspending and living above their means. I don't want you to be one of those people. Spending is fine, but *excessive* spending is not. The simplest concept to live by in order to keep your spending in check is "spend less than you earn."

Dear Amber,

In today's world of apps for your smart phone, I must say that there are many that will make you a wiser spender. A few of my favorites are the ones that let you know weeks in advance about the Black Friday sales, access your bank accounts and deposit checks by simply photographing them, find the closest ATM for your bank, find the cheapest place to get a prescription filled, trade stocks; and the one I love the most is the gas app that shows you the cheapest gas in your area. There are hundreds more, so take advantage of what technology has to offer that could actually help you save a little money.

Love,
One happy-app Mom

*   *   *

Dear Amber,

I think you have learned this lesson at a young age, so I guess you are not completely ignoring me in your teenage years. When you go shopping, always start with the clearance racks, which are usually located at the back of the store. Retail is a quickly rotating business, and what happens with any merchandise at a store is that it either sells out, goes on sale, or gets marked clearance. If it sells out, it was not meant to be. If it goes on sale, you can consider it, and once it is marked clearance, it's calling your name. Most clothes go on clearance way before they go out of style.

Also, if you buy at the end of the season, you'll get super deals. Want a new pair of boots? Buy them in March. Want a new coat? Buy it in April. Want a new pair of sandals? Buy them in September. Want a new swimsuit? Buy it in October. You will save a ton of money.

Love,
Shopaholic Mom

*   *   *

Dear Amber,

Never buy an extended warranty on any products including appliances, TVs, and yes, even a car. These warranties are highly profitable for the companies that issue them for one good reason: people pay for them but rarely get to use them. On the rare occasion that you may actually need to use the warranty, there are so many "gotchas" that your warranty claim may be denied. They can say that you misused the product, did not follow manufacturer's guidelines for proper maintenance and care, or one of the other hundred things listed in the fine print on the warranty contract.

Warranties are nothing more than a huge moneymaker for the companies at the expense of consumers. So instead of giving the money to someone else for your peace of mind, give the money to yourself. Here is what I mean: just save the money you think you'll need for the product (mainly a car) in case something breaks down that you need to pay for. If nothing ever breaks down, then guess what? You keep the money and do whatever *you* want to.

Love,
Anti-warranty Mom

*   *   *

Dear Amber,

Don't let the big banks take advantage of you with stupid fees and penalties. But make sure you note that it is the fees and penalties that are stupid, not the banks. They make millions of dollars every year by taking advantage of consumers that do not manage their accounts properly.

Make sure you always have enough money to cover what is coming out, and avoid the fees that your bank is always waiting in the wings to charge you. Now I'm not suggesting that you keep one of those old-fashioned paper check registers; however, you can set up alerts, use your bank's app on your smartphone or check your account online regularly.

There are a few banks and credit unions that may have limited fees, but there is always some sort of fees you could be hit with if you don't keep up with what's going on with your account. Just take a good look at the chart of common fees you should look out for.

Love,
Mom for the reform of the morally compromised

Common Bank Account Fees (you should avoid)

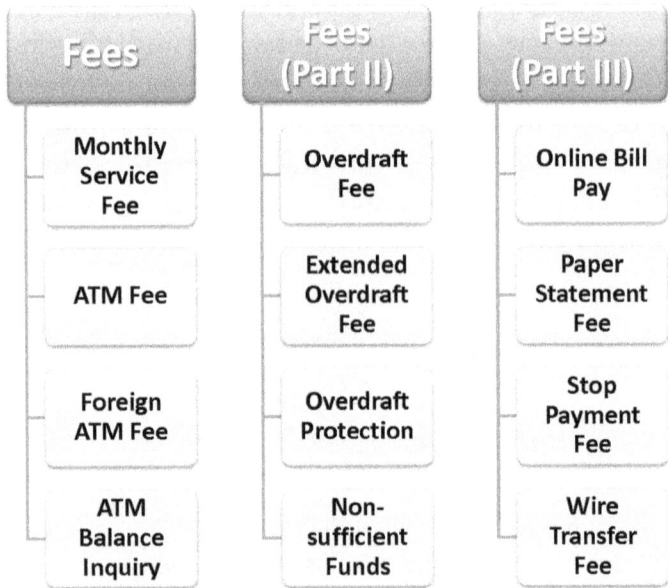

Fees	Fees (Part II)	Fees (Part III)
Monthly Service Fee	Overdraft Fee	Online Bill Pay
ATM Fee	Extended Overdraft Fee	Paper Statement Fee
Foreign ATM Fee	Overdraft Protection	Stop Payment Fee
ATM Balance Inquiry	Non-sufficient Funds	Wire Transfer Fee

* * *

Dear Amber,

Speaking of bank fees, be careful about using ATMs located inside some of the hotels near the theme parks in Orlando. In

2011, I stayed at one that had an ATM that charged $3.95 per transaction, and you could only get a maximum of $100 at a time; what a rip off! I later went just across the street to the theme park, and the fee for the ATM there was half the cost and had a much higher limit that you could withdraw per transaction.

Love,
ATM-fee-hating Mom

* * *

Dear Amber,

When you go to buy a car, never wait to get financing at the dealership! They know that if you have not prepared and arranged for financing prior to coming to their lot, you're a desperate or impulse buyer. They will typically charge you a much higher rate than you could probably get at a bank or credit union and charge you fees you may not have otherwise had to pay. The most ridiculous fee is an early termination fee, where, if you pay the loan off early, they make you pay an extra charge. Car dealerships not only make money from selling cars, but they also make money from selling loans for banks.

Now, even on the slim chance the dealer offers you a lower rate than what you've already arranged, you can still take it. As a matter of fact, be sure to mention the low rate that you have already been approved for with your bank or credit union, and give them the opportunity to beat it. Having choices is great!

Oh, and I forgot to mention that car dealerships will push you hard to get an extended warranty and become very aggressive about it, but don't fall for it.

You should have your mind made up already before you step on the dealer's lot: *You will get financing before going to the dealer. You will not buy an extended warranty. And you will walk away if you don't get the deal you want.* Now, let's repeat that so you'll be sure to remember it: *You will get financing before going to the dealer. You will not buy an extended warranty. And you will walk away if you don't get the deal you want.*

Love,
Desperateless-car-buying Mom

*   *   *

Dear Amber,

I wasn't always so smart when it comes to getting a car loan, so I wanted to share with you a mistake I made not so long ago. In 2006, I purchased a preowned luxury SUV for about $32,000, and the only option I considered for financing was through the dealership. I don't know why I didn't shop around for the best rate before; just stupid, I guess.

Anyway, I got a horrible deal on the loan at that dealership. My interest rate was 7.74%; there was a loan origination fee of $175 and an early termination fee of $150. By the way, the finance guy at the dealership lied to me about the early termination fee and told me there was none. I suppose I should have looked on the back of the loan agreement that noted this information in a four-point light-gray font, which seemed to almost blend into the paper. But I digress.

Looking back, with my credit score (which was about a 760 at the time), I know I could have found a loan for about 4% or less with none of those silly fees from a bank or credit union. The dealership wrote the loan for a big national bank, and I know they probably got a huge kickback at my expense. I would have saved about $3,000 in interest charges if I just would have shopped around to get the best deal on my car loan.

Love,
Mom with a car financing epiphany

*   *   *

Dear Amber,

When you are negotiating the price of a car, never, ever, pay sticker price (even if you go against my stern warning about buying a new one). Always know that the salesperson needs to sell you a car way more than you need to buy one. The salesperson has a monthly quota, a manager breathing down his or her neck, and wants to keep his job. So the best thing to do is make him feel like he is about to close the sale (get him salivating) and then walk away and say you'll think about it. I can almost guarantee you that he will sweeten the deal, especially when he figures out that he's not making his monthly sales quota. In the meantime, keep shopping around.

If you are trading in an old car for a new one, you do not have to let the salesperson know that up front—you should negotiate these two things separately to minimize the games. Once you do decide that you are ready to buy the car, always ask for a little something extra out of their dealership store, like new mats, laptop bag, umbrella; and they should be happy to do it. Oh, and it is okay to play car dealers against each other, especially with the ability to search for cars online.

Love,
Mom not afraid to stand her ground

*   *   *

Dear Amber,

Before purchasing a preowned car, it is mandatory (by Mom) that you get a certified mechanic to look at it and make sure it's in good running condition and not a lemon (this is called a prepurchase inspection). It'll cost you about $75-$150 to get this done, but it's money well spent. You can find a nearby certified mechanic at www.aaa.com, www.ase.com, or just google *prepurchase inspection* and the location of the vehicle.

Your first car was a 2003 Volkswagen Jetta in great condition, and we paid about $7,500 for it. That same car, brand new, would cost about $23,600 (hmmm . . . about 70% off, right?).

I have an exercise that I did to show you how fast a new car can go down in value (called depreciation) and make it more affordable for you once it's a few years old. I used your Volkswagen Jetta as an example, but you can do this exercise yourself on any vehicle by using one of the car valuation sites like www.kbb.com, www.edmunds.com, or www.nada.com and when shopping for the car you want online.

Estimated Depreciation of Volkswagen Jetta				
Model Year	Age of Vehicle	Average Sale Price	% of Value Lost	Your Savings
2012	New	$23,600	---	---
2011	1 year old	$18,300	22%	$5,300
2010	2 years old	$17,800	25%	$5,800
2009	3 years old	$16,300	31%	$7,300
2008	4 years old	$14,000	41%	$9,600
2007	5 years old	$12,500	47%	$11,100
2006	6 years old	$11,000	53%	$12,600

So you can buy a new 2012 Volkswagen Jetta for $23,600 and have it depreciate by almost 25% in the first year and almost 50% in the first five years or get one a few years old in very good condition for thousands of dollars less. You choose.

Love,
Like-new Mom

*   *   *

Dear Amber,

When you are ready to buy another vehicle and trade in your old one, be sure to do your homework before you go to the dealership. This will put you in a much better negotiating position by knowing what your car is worth as a trade-in to the dealer and about what you should pay for the car that you want. The most common websites that will give you the value of vehicles is www.kbb.com, www.edmunds.com, and www.nada.com. Between the three of these sites, you can come up with estimates very easily. Also, do a little online shopping for cars at sites like www.cars.com, www.autotrader.com, and www.carsforsale.com.

As soon as you let the salesperson at the dealership know the homework that you have done and that you know what you are talking about, he or she will cut the crap and be less likely to play games with you. Knowledge is power.

Love,
Mom doing her homework

*   *   *

Dear Amber,

When you are doing your research for purchasing a car, another thing you should do is consider the safety aspects. You can do that by going to www.safecar.gov, which is a government website dedicated to the safety aspects of vehicles including ratings, complaints, crash test reports, defects, and recalls. My favorite part of this site is that you can sign up to receive e-mail alerts on any recalls for your vehicle. I know how you love the easy button, so this is one of them. Prior to purchasing the car you want, it wouldn't hurt to find out if there were any recalls on the vehicle, and if so, make sure they were fixed.

Love,
Easy-to-recall Mom

*   *   *

Dear Amber,

Competition is the consumer's BFF. With most things that you have in life, you'll be able to get it from more than one company; in fact, you'll have many choices. All those companies will want your business, and they compete against each other very aggressively. You being in the middle will benefit from one company trying to have a lower price, better product, or better service over their competitors. They want you to spend your money with them.

So take advantage of this position and always shop around; shoot, even play the companies against each other. If you do this, you will almost always come out with a better deal when you are shopping for things like mortgages, cell phone service, banking services, cars, hotels, utilities, appliances, groceries, etc. One time, when I was much younger, I decided I wanted to get my credit card interest rates down, so I called all five of the companies. I told them that I have five cards but was only going to keep three of them. The three I kept would be the ones with the lowest interest rate, so two would be eliminated. Do you know that all five companies lowered my rate? None of them wanted to lose a customer.

Love,
Mom that loves a good race

*   *   *

Dear Amber,

When you need to purchase something at a particular store, always check on the Internet to see if there are any discounts or coupons you can use. Just go online, and search the name of the retailer along with the word *coupon* or *promo*. By doing this, I've gotten coupons for Lowe's, Home Depot, Best Buy, and many other retailers to use online or in their store.

Love,
Scouring-for-coupons Mom

* * *

Dear Amber,

When you want to get a new TV, refrigerator, sofa, or any other household item, please avoid the "rent to own" places. They are about as bad as the Payday loan places, except they lend merchandise instead of money and have employees with bigger muscles so they can repossess your stuff if you don't pay.

If you do the math of what the "rent to own" places charge you every week to rent the item before you own it, you will end up paying three or four times what you would pay to just buy it out right. If you miss a payment, they will take the item back, which means you are out the money and the merchandise. If you don't have all the money you need to purchase the item, try saving up for it, use a low interest credit card or get a 0% interest for twelve months offer, and be sure to pay it off before the offer is over.

So don't be a fool to the "rent to own" stores; there are plenty of other people not as smart as you that will keep them in business.

Love,
Not-your-rent-to-own Mom

* * *

Dear Amber,

There will be many things that come your way claiming that you can earn a quick buck from doing almost nothing. Most of these types of things are designed to actually take your money one way or the other and make someone else rich. They're probably scams. If it sounds too good to be true, it probably is. Although I give you these words of wisdom, I know that you always like some concrete source to reference. So if you want to check out to see if some wonderful deal really is legitimate, just go online and enter the name of the company or deal, and put in the word *scam* behind it. You'll find all kinds of information from other people that may have been scammed, articles that may have been written, reviews from ratings websites, legal actions, and so on.

Love,
Suspicious Mom

*　　*　　*

Dear Amber,

When you need to get a prescription filled or transferred, remember that many drug or grocery stores offer $4 or less generics and $10-$25 coupons that can be found in their weekly ad or online (usually to be used on other items in the store). Many places also now offer to fill a prescription of certain antibiotics for free. Remember all those times you had to take that pink liquid, Amoxicillin? Well, that medication was always free when I got the prescription filled at Meijer.

The purpose of those very generous offers is because they know that most people stick with one place for all their prescriptions, so if they get you to come in once, you'll probably come there all the time. They're hoping to get all your future pharmaceutical business and over-the-counter stuff like shampoo, aspirin, etc. You will do better by going to the store that is offering the best incentive.

Oh, and don't forget to check online to see if the manufacturer of the drug you need has any special incentives or discounts; you can usually use those on top of what is offered at the store. Just search for the name of the manufacturer and drug.

I hate even talking about you ever being ill, but my hope is that you will be as wise with your money when you are sick as you are in good health.

Love,
Healthy Mom

*   *   *

Dear Amber,

Whenever you have to see a doctor, he or she will often prescribe medication for your ailment. You should first always ask the doctor to prescribe a medication with a generic equivalent if it is available. You ask for this first because using generics will give you the greatest savings, even if you do not use insurance (you can get many generics for $4).

Secondly, if there is no generic equivalent for the medication, ask the doctor if they have any free samples that you can take with you. Most doctors are happy to do this, especially if you have been a patient of theirs for a while. You see, many drug companies will give free samples to the doctor in hopes that they will prescribe their brand over another. The doctors often just keep the free samples around until someone asks for them, or they expire. This could help you save on your prescription if you have a plan where you pay a percentage of the cost of the medication. The free samples will already be a portion of the total amount of the medication your doctor prescribed. So you may only need to get part the prescription filled at the pharmacy.

Please don't be shy about asking your doctor these things. They are well aware of the consumer need for affordable prescription drugs, and most are happy to help if you just ask. Consider it a part of the doctor/patient relationship and the service they provide as medical professionals.

Love,
Mom pushing for affordable drugs

*   *   *

Dear Amber,

Hopefully in your younger years, you will not encounter many dealings with your health insurance, but it is something you need to have because the cost of health care for major medical issues can be outrageously expensive. Most employers offer health insurance plans to their employees, and the company pays a portion of the cost of the plan (called a premium). The premiums for your employer-sponsored health insurance will probably be taken directly out of your paycheck before you see it.

As a young person, you will generally be a low consumer of health care, so I recommend that you choose a high-deductible health insurance plan. A deductible is the amount you pay out of your pocket before your insurance will kick in. A typical traditional health insurance plan for an individual might not have a deductible or a very low one, say $400 per year, and you still pay for a portion of your health care services. A high-deductible plan will have a much higher deductible, like $1,200 per year for an individual plan, but this type of plan will almost always have the lowest cost premium.

So here's the kicker: if you only go once a year for an annual physical, which probably cost less than $200 (but usually is free with a high-deductible plan) and only other minor medical services, why pay the higher premiums?

One of the best benefits with the high-deductible plans is that you are allowed to set up what is called a health savings account (HSA) and make pretax contributions for future medical expenses.

When you are ready to use the money in that account for qualified medical expenses, the money you take out is also tax free.

The money you put in your HSA can be rolled over from year to year, and once it gets to a certain amount, you may be allowed to invest the money you have accumulated (just like a 401(k)). The HSA individual contribution limit for 2012 is $3,100, so you could really rack up some tax advantaged money in this account. You can go to the Internal Revenue Service website (www.irs.gov) for more information about HSAs and how you can use them.

Love,
High-deductible Mom

*   *   *

Dear Amber,

Speaking of health care, it's become almost impossible to find the true cost of medical services. The insurance companies pretty much run the game, and most doctors and health providers hate dealing with them as much as we do.

Most medical bills only show you a code that consumers have no clue about and a brief description that seem to only be listed for the benefit of insurance company. So trying to figure out what you are being charged for, what portion your insurance picked up, and if the bill is correct is a ridiculous process. Now I'm not saying that the insurance companies are lying, cheating, unscrupulous entities; but you gotta wonder why they maintain a system that is so incomprehensible.

One doctor did do something about this and created a great website that uncovers a lot of the hidden and inflated costs with medical billing and insurance companies. The website is www.truecostofhealthcare.org, written by David Belk, MD. If I lived in San Francisco, this guy would be my doctor!

Love,
Mom sick of bad behavior by the healthcare industry

*   *   *

Dear Amber,

At some point you will need to shop for car insurance. So I wanted to make sure you understood the three basic types of coverage:

Liability. This coverage pays for third-party personal injury and death-related claims, as well as any damage to another person's property that occurs as a result of your automobile accident. Liability coverage is required in all but a few states.

Collision. This coverage pays to repair your car after an accident. It is required if you have a loan against your vehicle because the car isn't really yours—it belongs to the bank, which wants to avoid getting stuck with a wrecked car.

Comprehensive. This coverage pays for damage incurred as a result of theft, vandalism, fire, water, etc. If you paid cash for your car or paid off your car loan, you may not need collision or comprehensive coverage.

Love,
Mom covering her assets

*   *   *

Dear Amber,

Insurance is designed to protect your home and car from damage, but when an accident happens, you need to pump your breaks before filing a claim. Why? Because, as silly as it may seem, the decision to file a claim will likely increase your insurance rates in the future. This is true even if the accident was minor or was not your fault (like it never is). The logic of the insurance company is that after you file a claim, you are a greater risk and should have to pay more money to them. So remember: the greater the number of claims filed, the greater the likelihood of a rate hike. And in a worst case scenario, if you file too many claims, the insurance company may not renew your policy (good luck trying to find a decent policy with another company).

A good rule to follow is to only file a claim in the event of catastrophic loss (a really big one). If your car gets a dent on the bumper or a few shingles blow off the roof on the house, you may be better off to take care of the expense on your own (another good reason to keep an emergency fund). On the other hand, if your car is totaled in an accident or the entire roof of your house caves in, filing a claim will make more sense. Just keep in mind that even though you have coverage and have paid your premiums on time for years, filing the claim will still likely affect your future insurance rates.

Love,
Mom pausing before a claim

* * *

Dear Amber,

As you shop for car and home insurance, you will find that it can be very expensive. So here are some discounts that most insurance companies offer:

Car

- Job tenure
- College degree
- Alarm system
- Distance from work
- Total miles driven per year
- VIN etched in glass
- Employer discount
- Garaged vehicle
- Defensive driving course
- Multiple policies

- High credit score
- High GPA
- Always ask the question, What other discounts do you offer?

Home

- Multiple policies
- Job tenure
- College degree
- Theft deterrent (alarm system)
- Employer discount
- Fire extinguisher
- Close proximity to fire station
- Close proximity to fire hydrant
- High credit score

Love,
Wisely-insured Mom

* * *

Dear Amber,

I gave you a list of many discounts that you could get on your car and home insurance, but I also want to mention a few other ways to further reduce the cost of your home and car insurance:

Shop around. Insurance companies are very competitive, and they all claim to be the lowest. So make sure you shop around and get the lowest possible rate. Remember that competition is your BFF.

Increase your deductible. Normally the insurance company will start you out with the lowest possible deductible (usually around $250 for a car or $500 for a home) that actually costs you the most. If you raise your deductible (to around $1,500 or $2,500 for a home), the premiums for your insurance will go down. Remember, the higher your deductible, the lower the cost of your premium. Sure, you will have to pay a little more out of pocket in the unlikely event you would have to file a claim, but that is just another reason to keep an emergency fund. The money you save on your annual premium will probably far outweigh the deductible you might have to pay if you have to file a claim.

Drop your collision coverage. If your car is paid for, you are only required to have liability insurance in most states so you can drop the collision or comprehensive part of your insurance. This will reduce the cost of your insurance premium for your car. Typically, if the car is paid off, the value is low and may not be as much of a hardship for you to fix or replace yourself. I would say, if the car is worth less than $6,000 and is paid for, consider dropping the collision and comprehensive insurance and use the money you save on your premium to save for a down payment on another car.

Lower the amount of liability coverage. The insurance company will likely have this as a higher amount than you need. The higher the liability amount, the higher the cost of the premium.

Love,
Mom reducing waste

*   *   *

Dear Amber,

When it comes to insurance, remember that in most cases, you are able to switch companies at any time. You are not locked into a long-term contract, which means you are a free agent. Even if you have prepaid for the year, the insurance company will more than likely cut you a prorated refund check. So if your insurance company is not treating you right or if you shop around and find that you are not getting the best deal, it's time to make a move.

Love,
Free-agent Mom

*   *   *

Dear Amber,

Buying a home is one of the biggest purchases that you will make in your life. There is a lot of research that your real estate agent will do for you, as they should because of the commission that they will get from selling the house to you (paid for by the seller). You should still do your own research.

One of the best things to know is the tax-assessed value of the homes that you are looking at. Most counties have online access where you can look up the assessed value of any home. Just go online and search the terms *tax assessor* and the name of the county and state where the home is located. It will show you exactly what the taxes were for the current year and previous years. You can see if the taxes and home value went up, down, or stayed the same each year. Some counties will even show you the last price each home sold for. Most of the county websites will allow you to search by address, but some will require what is called a parcel ID number. This parcel ID number may be on the listing for the home up for sale, or you could get that from your real estate agent.

There are many online resources that will allow you to find out about the schools, neighborhood, and even homeowner associations. You can also pull up maps that will show you a satellite view that allows you to zoom in so close, you can actually see the house you are looking for and all those around it. Using maps online, you can see what is near a home (like shopping malls, restaurants, schools, train tracks, etc.) that may impact your buying decision.

Doing a little research on your own will make you a wiser home buyer and put you in a better negotiating position. Knowledge is power.

Love,
Mom, staunch advocate for doing your own research

*   *   *

CHAPTER 3

Credit

How you manage credit becomes a part of your credit history, which will be relied upon again and again throughout your life. Although your credit history has traditionally been used by lenders when you want to borrow money or get a credit card, that is not all it's used for today. Now, credit scores and reports are used by many insurance companies, employers, and other businesses as part of their decision-making process. So good credit is not only a crucial part of your financial well-being but can also have an impact on other parts of your life. Credit can be your best friend or your worst enemy.

Dear Amber,

Credit cards are not a bad thing, but the way many people manage them can be. People get into trouble using credit cards because of mismanaging the privilege and allowing the credit card companies to penalize them with high fees, large penalties, and excessive interest rates.

So it's okay to use credit cards, but you must follow "Mom's Top 5 Credit Card Rules" to be the winner in the game:

Mom's Top 5 Credit Card Rules

Rule #1
- Only charge what you can pay off in full every month, before the due date

Rule #2
- Get a credit card with a sign up bonus, great perks and no annual fee

Rule #3
- Get a low interest rate (for the rare occasion that you may have to carry a balance)

Rule #4
- Manage your spending throughout the month and charge only what you can pay off

Rule #5
- If you can't pay off what you charged in full in a given month, refer to **Rule #1**

One note, the credit card companies will not like you if you follow these rules because they don't make much money off your account. Fortunately for the credit card companies, most people don't follow these rules, and they make gobs of money.

Love,
Mom that loves golden rules

*   *   *

Dear Amber,

I know that you have wondered if the 0% interest rate for 12 months (or sometimes longer) balance transfer credit card offers are too good to be true and how they make money off it. Well, baby, this is another instance where it's better to be in the minority. Here's how the credit card companies make money off these 0% offers:

- They know just about everyone will not pay off their balance by the 12th month
- If you don't pay the balance off in 12 months as agreed, you get hit with an interest rate of the bank's choosing—they make money
- If the credit card is paid late in any month, there is a fee, and you get penalized with an even higher rate—they make more money
- If you decided to use the card and go over the credit limit, they will let you because (you guessed it)—they more make money

Here's how *you* can make money off the credit card companies with this offer:

- Read all the small print first—what the **bold** print giveth, the *small* print taketh away.
- Make sure there is no transaction fee associated with the offer or a very low one, like 3% or less
- With a balance transfer, the bank simply provides you with balance transfer checks to use or sends the payment directly to another bank you request.
- Once you make the balance transfer, you have the bank's money free for 12 months; use it wisely (like pay off another high-interest-rate credit card).

- Make a plan to pay off the balance in 11 months instead of 12, just to make sure they have enough time to process that final payment and send you a $0 balance statement.
- The best way to make sure you don't forget when it's due is to add the due date to the name of the monthly bill pay account online; that way, every month you make a payment, you'll be reminded of when it's due.
- Do not use that card to make any purchases or other transactions that will incur interest. If you do, none of your monthly minimum payments will go toward the higher interest rates; they will go toward the 0% first (in favor of the credit card company), and you will pay interest on the balance with the higher rate. Common sense would say that your minimum payments would go toward the higher interest rate first, but it is just the opposite. Be sure to read my letter to you about how credit card payments are allocated.

If you want to find a good list of current 0% balance transfer offers, there are many websites dedicated to this, like Smart Balance Transfers (www.smartbalancetransfers.com).

Love,
Zero-percent Mom

*   *   *

Dear Amber,

I want to make sure you know about an alternative and easy way you can get cash when you need it without a fee. First of all, most credit card companies will charge you huge interest rates (that usually start to accrue as soon as you get the money) and transaction fees to take a cash advance to get money. Also, if you are not near an ATM that belongs to your bank, you'll have to pay a $2-$4 fee to the owner of the ATM you use and to your bank. That sucks! Instead, I would like you to get a Discover Card, which, I was happy to learn, lets you get cash over your purchase at many stores including Walmart, Kroger, and Meijer. Typically they will allow $60-$80 over the amount of your purchase, and you can find a complete list of the retailers that participate on their website (last I checked it was over 60).

When you make a purchase, you are asked if you want cash over, and you choose the amount (this may vary by the retailer). There is no fee, and you won't pay any interest on it if you pay off your balance each month like Mom taught you to always do. Once I got my Discover Card, I rarely had to go to the ATM again and just used the Discover cash over when I was already at the store (one less trip). I love easy.

Love,
Easy Mom

*   *   *

Dear Amber,

The frequent flyer programs have become a joke and not really worth considering when making buying decisions anymore. Way back in the day, I redeemed my miles for two round trip tickets to Europe for only 35,000 miles per ticket. These days, it would take two or three times that, and domestic flights aren't much better. I used to get credit cards and be very loyal to certain airlines to earn the miles in hopes of earning a free flight quickly. That worked for quite a while, but around 2008, all the airlines just jacked up the amount of miles required for a free flight. It's just not worth it anymore.

The airline cards are one of the few types of credit cards that make you pay an annual fee. I used to think it was worth the annual fee (about $95/year), but now I don't think it is wise to even bother because you don't get the pay off you used to. There are way too many credit cards out there that give you all kinds of awards and incentives that do not charge an annual fee, and I have many. My suggestion is "Don't pay an annual fee for a credit card" because you have too many better choices available to you.

Love,
No-more-million-miles Mom

* * *

Dear Amber,

When you are ready to travel abroad, you'll be spending lots of money. But you should know that just about every credit card charges what's called a *foreign transaction fee* of about 1%-4%. So add that to the exchange rate on all the things you will want to buy, and you'll pay way more than you thought. For example, if you spend $5,000 when you go to Europe and use a card with a 4% foreign transaction fee, you'll pay an additional $200 in fees on those purchases.

There are two credit cards I know of that do not charge a foreign transaction fee at all, and those are Pentagon Federal Credit Union (PenFed) and Capital One. If you did a little research, you may find a few others, most likely from a credit union or travel rewards card. So be sure you take a card that does not have a foreign transaction fee with you when you travel out of the country. Make sure you do your homework on this well in advance of your trip (don't wait until the day before!). Instead of giving your money to the credit card company for mindless fees; go buy yourself a new pair of designer shoes!

Love,
Mom with a great foreign policy

* * *

Dear Amber,

You'll probably have many credit cards during your lifetime for many different reasons, and these days they are almost a requirement. But it is also *my* requirement that you do the following when you use credit cards.

- Pay them off every month
- Get as many free perks and bonuses as you can
- Never pay an annual fee
- Never pay interest
- Never pay late fees
- Never pay over the limit fees
- Never pay foreign transaction fees
- Never pay a credit line increase fee
- And stay away from the other "gotchas" that credit card companies are notorious for

Okay, I know I'm rambling, but the reason for this letter is not to tear down credit cards; it's actually to tout my favorite one—Discover Card. Here's why: I got the card in the first place because of a 12-month, 0% interest balance transfer offer (of course, no transaction fee). With a balance transfer, they just give you a check, and you can deposit it into a checking account and use it any way you want. Pay it off within 11 months, giving you one month to spare, and you just got almost a 1-year, interest-free loan. I think they have better perks than most other credit cards (and I've had many). Sure they give you the 1% cash back like many other cards, but that's not all. Several times during the year, they give you the chance to earn 5% cash back on certain categories like groceries, gas, travel, etc.

I even received one promotion that gave me a $250 bonus! All I had to do is charge a certain amount each month (below what I normally charge anyway) for 4 or 5 months in a row. So of course, what did I do? I used that Discover Card exclusively during that time, which is just what they want because they get fees from the merchant every time the card is used. So they win, and I win. The other thing I love about this card is that it lets me get cash over the amount of my purchase when I am at stores like Meijer and Walmart. I sometimes get $60 or $80 at a time (without a fee) and don't have to stop at the ATM. Again, there is no extra fee to pay in order to do this, so I just basically borrow their money for a few weeks, and it's treated just like a purchase. These features make the Discover Card my favorite and the one I use the most. The only thing that would make this better would be to remove the foreign transaction fee (I think they charge 3%) and to be more widely accepted (occasionally I find merchants that do not accept this card). Since this card meets most of Mom's requirements, this is the one I would recommend you have.

Love,
Mom playing her cards right

* * *

Dear Amber,

When you are looking to get a credit card, you have a lot of choices. If you have great credit (about 730 credit score or above), the credit card companies will beat a path to your mailbox. They'll try enticing you with incentives like 0% interest, sign-up bonus, rewards, and more. Take advantage of these offers, but make sure you always read the fine print and review the card member agreement, which gives you the important things you need to know before you open a credit card. A couple of good websites to use to find the type of credit card you are looking for is www.creditcards.com and www.smartbalancetransfers.com.

I would urge you to choose a card that does not charge an annual fee because there are so many options for great credit cards without a fee. There are many other credit card fees that you should be wary of, just take a look at the most common ones on the chart at the end of this letter.

Love,
Mom with high aspirations

Common Credit Cards Fees (you should avoid)

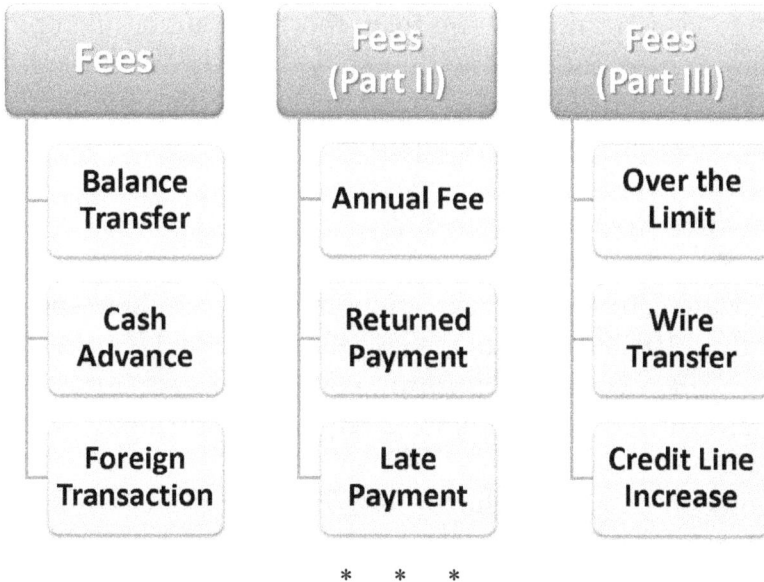

Fees	Fees (Part II)	Fees (Part III)
Balance Transfer	Annual Fee	Over the Limit
Cash Advance	Returned Payment	Wire Transfer
Foreign Transaction	Late Payment	Credit Line Increase

* * *

Dear Amber,

One of the most important things you need to know about credit is your credit report. This report compiles information about how you pay your debts and handle credit. It also keeps a record of all your credit accounts (current and past). There are three major credit reporting agencies that do this: *Experian, Equifax,* and *TransUnion.* When you apply for new credit, a report is pulled on you from one of these companies or possibly all three before you are granted the new credit.

You should be fully aware of everything that is on your credit report by checking it yourself for *free*. Federal law allows you to get your credit report once a year from each of three major credit reporting agencies at www.annualcreditreport.com.

Additionally, you're entitled to a free report if a company takes adverse action against you, such as denying your application for credit, insurance, or employment, and you ask for your report within sixty days of receiving notice of the action. The notice will give you the name, address, and phone number of the credit reporting agency.

You're also entitled to one free report if you are unemployed and plan to look for a job within sixty days, on welfare, or your report is inaccurate because of fraud, including identity theft.

You can request your free report through the following ways:

- *Online:* www.annualcreditreport.com
- *Phone:* 1-877-322-8228 (automated system)
- *Mail:* Annual Credit Report Request Services, PO Box 105281, Atlanta, GA 30348-5281. Here is a link to get a copy of the form you need to use: https://www.annualcreditreport.com/cra/requestformfinal.pdf

If you go online, be careful to only go to www.annualcreditreport.com to get your free report because there are a lot of fakes out there that will try to lure you to the wrong site and charge you for the credit report or other credit-related product (it's usually the ones with the catchy jingle). If you are asked for your credit card information, you know it's not free because they are going to bill you for something.

So in the spirit of remembering important things by repeating them again and again, like when you were in elementary school, remember this:

The *only* online resource authorized by federal law to get your free annual credit report is www.annualcreditreport.com.

The *only* online resource authorized by federal law to get your free annual credit report is www.annualcreditreport.com.

The *only* online resource authorized by federal law to get your free annual credit report is www.annualcreditreport.com.

Love,
Mom urging you to remember www.annualcreditreport.com

*   *   *

Dear Amber,

One of the most important numbers you will have in your life is your credit score. Similar to your GPA score in school, you will have this financial score in real life. A credit score assigns a number to your credit history which creditors use to judge your credit worthiness.

The most common credit score is your FICO, which stands for *Fair Isaac Corporation* score. Your FICO score ranges from 300-850. There are other credit scores out there, but the most used one is FICO. There is some general information about how your credit score is calculated, but in my opinion, it's treated like some big secret formula. Maybe that's why only about half of Americans even know what their credit score is. I think that there should be some federal standard calculator that can be used by consumers and creditors to figure the same score. Since that is probably a long time coming, make sure you always have a great credit score (730+) so that when you need new credit, it is not a problem. It is very simple to keep a good credit history, just follow these few things, and you'll have no problem:

1. Pay your bills early or on time.
2. On your credit cards, don't use more than 30% of your available credit.
3. Don't file for bankruptcy.
4. Don't have any judgments or liens against you.
5. Check your credit report regularly to correct any inaccuracies or issues.

Free FICO scores are available for active duty military personnel and their spouse at www.saveandinvest.org/MilitaryCenter.

For everyone else, there are a couple of websites that offer a very close estimate or simulations of your credit score for free, so I would start there before paying for the score elsewhere. Those are www.creditkarma.com and www.quizzle.com, which may have a few ads and offers but that is part of why it's free. To get your actual credit score, you will have to pay for it at www.myfico.com or one of the credit reporting agencies.

Love,
803-credit-score Mom

*   *   *

Dear Amber,

I must give kudos to www.creditkarma.com for having what I consider the best tools for analyzing and tracking your credit history. Credit Karma gives you a letter grade for your credit score and a scale that shows the zone you fall in (excellent, good, fair, poor, etc.).

They have a great website and app that help you track things like your debt-to-credit ratio, negative activities on your report, changes in your credit line, changes in an account status, and whole lot more that I just love.

The credit information on Credit Karma is provided by TransUnion, so it is just pulling from one of the three major credit reporting agencies. Even with that, Credit Karma has made it very easy for consumers to keep an eye on their credit, and I applaud that effort.

Love,
Mom supporting good credit karma

*   *   *

Dear Amber,

After you request your free credit report at www.annualcreditreport.com, you will likely find errors on it like the majority of people, including myself. Incorrect information on your credit report is very common and could include negative information that may affect your credit score and ability to obtain credit. It could also be an early sign of identity theft. So it is important to dispute and correct these errors when you become aware of them.

You know how I love to dispute, so let's get down to it! It is so much easier than most people think. I found the process to be fastest and easiest online because you simply click on the item you want to dispute and provide the necessary information. Also, you will get immediate confirmation that your dispute was received, and you can check the status of your request online. Even if you have a printed credit report, you can dispute it online by providing the credit report number (usually found at the top of the report). I filed online disputes for several incorrect addresses on my credit report, and it only took about two days to get them corrected. Now, if you have disputes with creditors, it will likely take longer, but remember that in most states, they only have thirty days to respond to your dispute. If the creditor does not respond in that thirty-day period, the dispute is resolved as you have requested.

Below are the links to each of the major credit reporting agencies dispute pages. Once you get to each of the websites, you'll be given step-by-step instructions on how to submit a dispute online, by phone, and by mail.

- www.investigate.equifax.com
- http://www.experian.com/disputes
- www.transunion.com/disputeonline

Love,
Mom not afraid of a good fight

* * *

Dear Amber,

I want you to take your credit score seriously because it is more important today than ever before in how it impacts your life. It used to only matter if you wanted credit, but now, companies use your credit score for a number of different reasons, including the following:

- Obtaining a loan
- Obtaining a credit card or credit line
- Renting a place to live
- Insurance (auto, life, home)
- Acquiring a cell phone
- Setting up utilities for your home (cable, Internet, electric, water, gas)
- Seeking employment

Love,
Mom with a great set of scores

* * *

Dear Amber,

As I mentioned before, exactly how credit scores are calculated seems to be some big secret recipe. So I'll come close by at least giving you a close estimate about how your score is compiled:

- 35%—Payment history (Are you paying your bills on time?)
- 30%—Available credit being used (Are you maxing out all your credit cards?)
- 15%—Length of credit history (How long have you had your credit?)
- 10%—New credit (How often are you applying for new credit?)
- 10%—Types of credit (Do you have a mix of credit like credit cards, student loan, car loan, mortgage?)

Credit Score Calculation

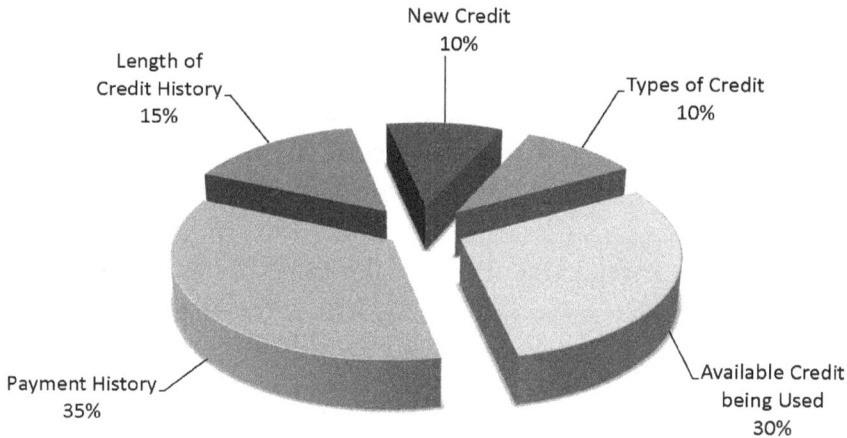

And if you want to try to prove me wrong, here are the things you can do that will really screw up your credit:

- Paying bills late
- Keeping too much debt
- Not paying the minimum amount required every month
- Having your credit cards maxed out
- Having too many inquiries within a year by applying for too many new credit accounts
- Not periodically checking your credit report
- Having your car repossessed
- Having a judgment or lien against your property
- Having a foreclosure or short sale on your home
- Filing for bankruptcy

Love,
Mom that just can't keep a secret

*   *   *

Dear Amber,

Don't ever take a cash advance on a credit card without knowing the hefty cost you'll pay for it. The interest rate to do this type of transaction is usually much more than making a purchase. Most cards will charge you about 20%-30% in interest, and you will be charged that rate from the first day you get the money out. Plus, they'll charge you a transaction fee of about 3%-5%.

So back to math class. If you take out a $400 cash advance, add a 5% transaction fee ($20) and 30% interest rate, and you're looking at over $30 just for the first month. If you didn't pay this off for a year, you could end up paying over $100 just in fees. That would suck! So please be smarter.

Love,
Mom staying away from things that just don't add up

*   *   *

Dear Amber,

When you get credit card offers in the mail, they will always highlight and bold the good things about the offer. This is not what is usually the most important to you. You should go straight to the small print (usually on the back page) and read the terms and conditions. This is what will tell you the *real* offer and the "gotchas." Normally, by the time I have read the fine small, the offer is in the trash. What the bold print giveth, the small print taketh away.

Love,
Forget-the-small-print Mom

*   *   *

Dear Amber,

I just wanted to explain the good, the bad, and the ugly when it comes to debit cards.

The Good. When you use a debit card, the money is coming directly from your checking account. You are not racking up charges that you might not be able to pay back later like you do with a credit card.

The Bad. If you don't have enough money in your account, the charge may be denied, or you will incur big fees if the transaction does go through. Banks now have to get your permission in order to overdraw your account with a debit transaction. They are happy to let you overdraw your account because they make big bucks from the fees they charge you. So if you used a debit card to pay for a $10 lunch at McDonald's, and you are overdrawn on your account, that transaction could end up costing you over $45. That's a very expensive lunch!

The Ugly. If your debit card is stolen and fraudulent charges are made, your money is gone. In order to get it back, you have to deal with the bank, prove that the charges were not yours, complete the paperwork, and possibly wait many months before you see a penny of your money. If you ever need to dispute a charge for other reasons such as bad service, you didn't get what paid for, etc., you have no recourse like you do with a credit card. Also, places like hotels and car rental agencies often put large holds on your account in advance of the transaction, which could cause you to bounce checks even though the money is there in your account.

With a debit card, you do not have the same rights as with a credit card when fraud and disputes are involved—with a credit card, it's much easier. Mom says, "Ditch the debit card, and use the credit card (wisely)."

Love,
Mom that knows not all cards are created equal

* * *

Dear Amber,

Good behavior with credit does put you in the driver's seat when it comes to dealing with creditors. If you always pay your credit card bill on time, but you happen to slip up one time, the credit card company will likely forgive the fees.

Just call them up and let them know you've been a loyal customer and always pay on time, but there was an oversight this time and you'd like them to reverse the charge. They'll put you on hold for a few seconds to check over your account to make sure you are not a habitual late payer, and once they see that you are not, they come back on the phone and will say something like this in a very respectful way: "Ma'am, we'd be happy to reverse the charges, and thank you for being our customer." You are the type of customer that they want to keep. The same kind of scenario applies to checking accounts and their fees, car loans and their fees, utility bills and their fees, cell phone bills and their fees, cable bills and their fees, and so on.

Love,
Well-positioned Mom

* * *

Dear Amber,

If you follow the advice I have given you in my other letters, I know you will have good credit (probably unlike most of your friends and family). I want you to protect that good credit and not have it compromised by identity theft or other fraudulent activity.

To do this, you don't need to use one of the credit monitoring services you see advertised all the time. They charge you a hefty fee (typically around $20 per month), and you are only notified *after* the activity has taken place. The absolutely best way to protect yourself from fraudulent activity is a credit freeze. This prevents the three major credit bureaus—Experian, Equifax, and TransUnion—from giving out information on your credit report until you provide consent. The consent is usually in the way of a PIN number issued to you and allows you to temporarily "thaw" your credit for legitimate access to your information.

The cost for a credit freeze and thaw varies by state but typically ranges from $3-$10 per person per bureau. In most states, victims of ID theft with a valid police report can get a free credit freeze. Compare that to the ridiculous cost of $20 per month for the credit monitoring service.

With the credit freeze, it's like not letting the cat out of the bag to begin with, and credit monitoring is like trying to catch the cat after it's gotten out: proactive versus reactive. I'll let you make the final decision of which one makes the most sense.

Love,
Mom not scared of a freeze

*   *   *

Dear Amber,

When you have finally paid off a credit card and do not intend to use it anymore, you should *not* close the account. It is okay to put the card away and only use it occasionally (to keep it active), but do not close the account. Here's why: each credit card has an available credit line. Here's why: they don't want to trust you with more credit than they think you will pay back. If you close one of those accounts, your total available credit is reduced, and that may negatively affect your credit score. Here's why: when figuring your credit score, your debt-to-credit ratio is important. Here's why: a debt-to-credit ratio is how much debt you have versus available credit, and if you have too much outstanding debt versus available credit, that's not good. You should keep this ratio to about 20%; so back to math class:

If you have 4 credit cards with $2,000 available credit each, then your total available credit is $8,000. If you have charged $1,200, then that is 15% of your available credit (this is a great credit ratio). If you closed 2 of those cards, your available credit would then be reduced to $4,000, and the $1,200 balance that you have would now represent 30% of your available credit (this is getting toward the danger zone). If you closed 3 of the credit cards, your available credit would only be $2,000, and the $1,200 balance you have would represent well over half of your available credit (this is a huge red flag on your credit report) Get it?

The only reason I would recommend closing a card is if there is an annual fee. Even before you closed one of those down, I would suggest that you call the credit card company to see if they have a no-fee version of the card that you have—most of them do.

Love,
Mom that loved learning fractions and percentages

* * *

Dear Amber,

I want you to know that if you choose *not* to pay your credit card bill in full each month, you should know how your payments are allocated. You may have charges with different interest rates, and you would assume the credit card company would have your payments go toward your highest interest rates first (so you can pay off the charges that are costing you the most first). But that is not the case if you are making just the minimum payment. They are totally self-serving and want to make sure they make as much money off you as possible. That means they want to charge you as long as they can for higher interest rate charges and have those be the last ones paid off (making them more money). This is not in the bold or highlighted print when you first get the card, but it is stipulated in the card holder agreement (in very tiny, tiny print of course). In early 2011, there was a change in the law which now makes the credit card companies apply any payment above your minimum payment, to your highest interest rates first; but that is only when you pay *more* than your minimum payment. Now why the heck did there have to be a law passed before these credit card companies would do something like this to help the consumer?

If you don't believe me, just pull out the magnifying glass and look at the small print on your credit card agreement. Knowing that you probably won't do that, below is the agreement language from three different credit card companies stating how they apply your payments as of June 2011:

Credit Card Number 1

"We apply payments and credits at our discretion, including in a manner most favorable or convenient for us. Each billing period, we will generally apply amounts you pay that exceed the minimum payment due to balances with higher APRs before balances with lower APRs as of the date we credit your payment."

Credit Card Number 2

"We will apply your minimum payment to pay off lower-rate balances before paying off higher-rate balances. We will apply any portion of your payment in excess of your minimum payment to higher Annual Percentage Rate balances before lower ones."

Credit Card Number 3

"Generally, we will apply your minimum payment first to lower APR balances (such as Purchases) before balances with higher APRs (such as Cash Advances). Payments made in excess of the minimum payment will generally be applied to balances with higher APRs first before balances with lower ones."

So when you make just the minimum payment, it will take you forever to pay off your balance, but the banks will make lots of money off you. Please read my letter again about my rules of using a credit card.

Oh, and this message was *not* brought to you by the credit card industry.

Love,

Mom despising corporate greed and narcissism

*   *   *

Dear Amber,

Making only the minimum monthly payment on your credit cards will cost you a lot of money over time. If you cannot pay your credit card in full every month (meaning that you didn't follow my number 1 rule), try to at least pay more than the minimum. Most of the minimum payment is going toward your interest and barely chips away at your principal. It could take you many, many, many years to pay the balance off that way. Don't believe me? Just look at the chart in this letter.

If you had a balance of $8,750 and only paid the minimum payment of $219 per month, it would take you *25 years* to pay it off, and you will have paid over *$8,500 in interest!* That is insane! Compare that to making a payment of $299 ($80 more than your minimum) that would pay off the balance in just 3 years and save you thousands of dollars in interest.

Payoff of $8,750 in Credit Card Debt

Question: If you had a Credit Card Balance of $8,750, which would be the correct answer on how to best pay it off with the least amount of interest
   A. 25 year payoff as illustrated below
   B. 3 year payoff as illustrated below
   C. None of the above, you should have paid the card off every month and not carry a balance in the first place

25 Year Payoff	3 year Payoff
• 15% APR	• 15% APR
• Pay only required minimum payment of $219/month (2.5% of balance)	• Pay $299/month ($80/month over minimum payment)
• You will pay $8,507 in interest	• You will pay $2,209 in interest
• You will pay a total of $17,257	• You will pay a total of $10,959
	• Your savings in time and interest is 22 years & $6,298!

In the past, the credit card companies would *never* highlight this kind of information on your statement because they want you to pay as much as possible in interest, making them as much money as possible. The only reason they disclose this information at all now is because they were forced to by changes in the credit card laws in 2010.

Love,
Mom that didn't skip math class

* * *

Dear Amber,

Even with all the laws and guidelines designed to protect consumers, there are still some businesses that just won't follow the rules! So it is up to you to know your rights as a consumer of credit, and an act called the *Fair Credit Reporting Act (FCRA)* helps you do that. The FCRA promotes the accuracy, fairness, and privacy of information in the files of consumer reporting agencies. The FCRA is your friend; hit them up at www.ftc.gov/credit.

Love,
Mom supporting the pursuit of law and order

* * *

CHAPTER 4

Debt

As of 2012, the United States had a national debt of over $16 trillion and growing by millions more as I write these letters (by the way, your share is about $52,000)! Many people have unlimited wants with limited means and end up taking on more debt than they can handle. This became painfully evident in 2008 when America's consumer debt went into crisis mode, and that makes it a very important topic for your generation. So I want to make sure debt does not become a problem for you. Debt is fine, but *excessive* debt is not.

Dear Amber,

I know, occasionally as you learn about money, you will make some mistakes. Please make Mom and yourself proud by facing your money problems and take proactive steps to fix them quickly. Worrying every day about money is miserable. If you don't believe me, just ask your aunts, uncles, cousins, and probably most of your friends.

Love,
Mom, champion for financial peace

* * *

Dear Amber,

Student loans are one of the largest and most common types of debts that college students will face. Over recent years, student loan debt has grown to levels that outpace credit card debt for the first time in history. Since most student loan debt cannot be discharged in bankruptcy, this obligation can go on for more than twenty years before it's paid off or forgiven. If a student loan goes into default, it is possible for the creditor to garnish your wages or seize the money in your bank account to pay the debt—yuck!

So hopefully I have scared you enough to listen to a few ways that will keep you in check if you decide to rely on student loans to help you through college. I actually love and hate student loans at the same time. There is not much love in this letter, so be sure to read my next letter closely for the love part.

Love,
Mom with a love-hate student loan relationship (Part 1)

* * *

Dear Amber,

For you and many of your friends, student loans may be the means to help you go to college. Taking out a student loan is not a bad thing, and if done with forethought and planning, it could be one of the best decisions you make for your future. So here are a few of my suggestions on the right way to go about getting a student loan to help you finance your education:

If you have to take on a student loan, make sure it is a federal government loan (www.studentloans.gov) and not a private one.

Before taking a student loan, make sure you have exhausted all your other resources for college money that you *do not* have to pay back: grants, scholarships, fellowships, internships, work study, working part-time or full-time, parents contribution (out of the goodness of their hearts).

Keep the student loan to an amount that is in line with the salary you can expect to make in your career field once you graduate. For example, if you are going to medical school, and you have to take out $80,000 in student loans, you could probably pay that back with ease because your salary for that profession would allow you to do so. However, if you are going to be a teacher or social worker, your salary would be much lower, and $80,000 in student loan debt would be overwhelming.

You have many repayment options for student loan debts, the newest being the Income-Based Repayment Plan (www.ibrinfo. org). Make sure you know all your options, and if needed, work with the loan servicer to address any special situation. This will help you avoid any kind of default on the loan and keep you in good standing.

Student loans are reported to the credit agencies, so being in good standing and paying the loan on time every month will reflect positively on your credit report.

You know I am a huge advocate of knowing your rights in any situation, so once you do have a loan, make sure you know, understand, and exercise your rights as a student loan borrower.

Here's a few websites to help you do that: www.finaid.org, www.studentloanborrowerassistance.org and www.projectonstudentdebt.org.

Love,
Mom with a love-hate student loan relationship (Part 2)

*   *   *

Dear Amber,

When trying to pay off your debt, there are two ways you can prioritize: *financially* and *psychologically*. The financial strategy of paying off debt is the way that will cost you less money in interest and allow you to pay your debts off quicker. You start with your highest rate credit card and pay that off first (regardless of the balance) because that is the one that is costing you the most money in interest. The next debt to pay off is the next highest interest rate and so on. The psychological strategy makes you feel better by getting rid of the card that you can eliminate the quickest, which is usually the one with the lowest balance (regardless of the interest rate).

Here is what your payoff chart would look like using a financial strategy:

- $8,000 on credit card at 32% interest (This one is costing you the most money, so pay it off first.)
- $5,000 on credit card at 20% interest (This one has the next highest interest rate, so pay it off next.)
- $1,500 on credit card at 8% (This one is costing you the least, so pay it off last.)

Here is what your payoff chart would look like using a psychological strategy:

- $1,500 on credit card at 8% (This has the lowest balance, so pay it off quickly and start feeling better.)

- $5,000 on credit card at 20% (Now you only have 2 cards to pay off; tackle this one next because it has the next lowest balance, you'll feel even better.)
- $8,000 on credit card at 32% (Ahhh, the last card to pay off, only one card away from your hallelujah moment.)

Regardless of which payoff strategy you use, you have accomplished the same goal of paying off your debt with some thought and strategy. I will help you celebrate either way.

Oh, I have one other quick note as you pay off your credit card debt. You should cut the cards up and never use them again unless you can pay off the balance each month. You should keep the credit line open though, if it is not too tempting. If you close the accounts, it could negatively affect your credit score because you are reducing your available credit.

Love,
Mom showing you two great routes to the same destination

*   *   *

Dear Amber,

Even if you have tried your hardest but end up having to file for bankruptcy, remember this: there are two types of debt that are typically not dischargeable (you can't blow this one off with the bankruptcy). Those are student loan debts and IRS debts. During a bankruptcy, you will have to account for all the money you have, and it will go toward your debt. The big exception here is that you will get to keep any retirement accounts and possibly other limited assets. Before you ever even think about bankruptcy, please give Mom a chance to help you with alternatives—I promise to give you a free pass on this one and not lecture you as you would have expected.

Love,
Mom against bankruptcy

*   *   *

Dear Amber,

Stay away from debt consolidation companies. Most of them are scams, and the ones that are not have very questionable practices that do not have the consumer's best interest in mind. Their top priority is to get you to pay a hefty fee up front (adding even more to your debt). If they get this fee, there is a small chance they will try to negotiate with your creditors to get your debts lowered (usually after convincing you to stop paying your creditors). This is something you can do yourself for free. Most old debts can be settled for about 50¢ on the dollar, but I would start with about 25¢. Settling a debt for less than you owe will reflect negatively on your credit report and temporarily hurt your credit score. Additionally, you will likely have to pay taxes for the amount your creditor forgave. I don't like this, but it's much better than filing for bankruptcy.

Love,
Mom that doesn't like to be played with

*   *   *

Dear Amber,

If you have old debts that are unpaid, you will likely hear from a debt collector. Debt collection companies basically buy old debts from banks or other creditors for pennies on the dollar in hopes of collecting more money from you than they had to pay to buy the debt. So these companies have a lot of wiggle room when it comes to settling the debt with you.

I would say, start with about 25¢ on the dollar (they will still probably be making a profit) and maybe ending up somewhere around 50¢ on the dollar. Let them know that you are willing to pay, but you don't have what they are asking for. Give them a lump sum amount that you can pay right now, and they will eventually accept it. Time is on your side; they want to settle the debt quickly, and you just want to wear them down. Ask your aunt Gwen, and she can tell you everything you ever wanted to know about dealing with debt collectors; she doesn't just play one on TV, she is one!

Love,
Mom against crumb snatchers and scavengers

*　　*　　*

Dear Amber,

Please, please, please, never get desperate enough for money where you need to go to a cash advance or payday loan place that you always see in strip malls (usually along with the bail bond places). Why? They count on people that have made the poorest money decisions with nowhere else to go that will do business with them, often because of bad credit or other issues. Because they are a last resort, they know they can charge whatever they want in interest.

There are regulations that have limited the interest rates these places can charge and several states that have even banned these types of loans.

Even though they are designed to be short-term loans, many people do not pay the loans on time and end up paying well over the interest rate and fees stated at the initiation of the loan. As I was writing this letter to you, I went online to one of those places to check the rates, and here is what I found for a $1,000 loan done on their website:

- 14-day loan originated in the state of Ohio
- $262 loan fee
- 683% APR

Sample Payday Loan Terms

$1,000
Online
Payday Loan
(Originated in Ohio)

14
Days

$262
Loan Fee

683%
APR

I didn't raise a fool, so I know you would never give away your hard-earned money this way.

Love,
Mom with a bad attitude toward predators

*   *   *

Dear Amber,

Some people in life are just not nice, like most collection agents. They sometimes will scare people into paying their debts (or debts of others) by using very aggressive, unethical, and sometimes, illegal tactics. You are too smart to be one of their victims. The best way is to just pay your debts. But if somehow you become a target of a collection agency, you have many rights under a federal law called the *Fair Debt Collection Practices Act (FDCPA)*. For instance, a debt collector must send you a written letter containing all the information about your debt within five days of speaking with you, so always ask for that (sometimes the debt may not even be yours!). For more information about the rights you have under this law, go to www.ftc.gov.

Also, if you send a written request to the collection agency, requesting to stop contacting you, they have to comply. If they call you after receiving the letter, they are in violation of the law. So even though I think not paying your debts is a money sin, you still deserve to be treated fairly and stand up for your rights.

Love,
Mom knowing that a bully, once confronted, always backs down

*   *   *

Dear Amber,

In your younger years, you may have many friends that are in the military who are proudly serving our country, just like your two cousins and uncle did. You should, first of all, always thank them for their service.

Also, they may appreciate you passing on some information that could save them some money. As a member of the armed forces, they have a special benefit that limits the amount they can be charged for interest to just 6% on credit cards, loans, and other debts that were incurred prior to serving. This is just one of the many provisions under a federal law called the *Servicemembers Civil Relief Act (SCRA)*, formally known as the Soldiers' and Sailors' Civil Relief Act. The SCRA offers a wide range of protections for the civil obligations of military men and women.

To get this benefit, the individual needs to request the interest rate reduction in writing (it would be wise to note that it's in accordance with federal law), along with a copy of their military orders to each of their creditors. It is also a good idea to follow up with a phone call to make sure the information was received. After receiving the notice, the creditor must reduce the interest rate to a maximum of 6%, effective the first day of active duty. This 6% rate only applies to debts incurred *before* serving active duty.

All the information about this and other benefits of the SCRA can be found at www.military.com/benefits or other resources available to you from the US Armed Forces.

Love,
Mom proudly waving a yellow ribbon

*   *   *

Dear Amber,

Here's a letter to just share with you something stupid that I did with money when I was young and didn't know better. When I was working my way through college, I decided to go out and buy a new car (yes, a new one and not a used one!). I thought that you could not negotiate the price of a new car (mistake number 1) and that you had to pay sticker price. Of course, the car salesman didn't tell me any different, and yes, I listened to what he said (mistake number 2). I just had to have that brand-new electric blue Ford Probe.

I was glad at the time that the dealership financed a loan for me because I had not made any financing arrangements on my own (mistake number 3). I only had to put about $200 down, and my payments were $326 per month for five years (mistake number 4). I don't even think I ever asked what the interest rate was on the loan. Over $300 a month was pretty steep for a college student only making about $11,000 a year, but I figured, if they thought I couldn't afford it, they would not have given me the loan (mistake number 5)—they were the experts and had to know what they were doing. At the end of the day, I was so proud to have a brand-new car.

Fast forward about a year, I finally realized that I could barely make the monthly payments and hardly had any money left over each month to do anything else. I just could not do it anymore. So I went to the bank to try and refinance the car loan and hopefully get lower payments that I could afford. I was very scared going in there because I didn't know what to expect. The person at the bank pulled up the information on my car and, point blank, told me that there was no way they could refinance the car because I owed way more on it than it was worth. I was crushed! I just slithered out of the bank, got into my $326 per month car, and started crying. I didn't know what to do. I had very little money and was still stuck with paying $326 per month for this car, on top of my tuition, food, and rent. I did manage to scrape up the payments each month (with no help from anyone else by the way). To this day, I don't know how in the heck I did it, but I paid that car off in five years as agreed. It took me longer to pay that loan off than it did to get through college. After that, I vowed to never *ever* be that stupid! Mom makes mistakes too.

Love,
Foolish Mom

* * *

Dear Amber,

These days, one of the best places to do your banking is a credit union. Credit unions are owned by their members, and their customers are their members! They usually have much better interest rates on their loans and other banking services. You can find a list of credit unions at www.ncua.gov. I think one of the best credit unions is *Pentagon Federal Credit Union* (www.penfed. org). In 2012, they offered used car loans at 1.49% APR for up to 60 months, when other lenders were charging as much as 12% or more for a shorter term loan.

Yes, credit unions limit who can join (like who you work for or where you live), but they are not as restrictive as you would think and have become much more open to who can join. Pentagon Federal Credit Union is traditionally for the military and other federal workers, but I joined in 2012! Little did I know, they have other eligibility options, including joining a nonprofit military organization (open for anyone to join) for a $20 membership fee that is tax deductible and supports our troops. Doing two good things at once never hurts!

Love,
Mom applauding credit unions

* * *

Dear Amber,

When you need to borrow money, you have so many options (the better your credit, the more options you have). Your first thought will probably be to go to one of the big banks that you see advertised on TV and the Internet all the time. Those should not be at the top of your list because they rarely have the best rates and their customer service often sucks (just take a look at some of the consumer rating websites).

As I mentioned in my previous letter, my favorite place for loans and other financial services is credit unions (proudly owned by the members they serve). Most have much better rates than the big banks and even better customer service. To me this is a great set up!

To help you decide the best place to go when you need a car, home, personal, or other type of loan, take a look at this guide I put together just for you on the best place to get a loan.

Love,
Loan-broker Mom

Mom's Guide to Where to get a Loan

BEST
Credit Union
Online Bank
Community/Regional Bank

OKAY
National Bank

WORST
Family & Friends

NEVER!
NEVER!
NEVER!
Payday Loan

*   *   *

Dear Amber,

I wanted to talk to you about 401(k) loans. Most information you will find on this topic highly discourages this primarily because it takes your money out of the market and doesn't get the growth you would have otherwise been earning on your investments. That is true. *However*, I think it can be a wonderful option if you clearly understand all the rules and use this option sparingly (and not as a piggy bank to keep paying off something like reoccurring debt).

A 401(k) loan is where you borrow money from your employer-sponsored 401(k) retirement account. There is no credit approval or bank loan application to fill out because you are really borrowing from yourself. It is your money, and if you have been wise enough to save for your retirement, then you should be commended for that. Many employers do allow you to borrow from your 401(k) with some restrictions.

When you pay back your 401(k) loan, you do have to pay interest on it, but that interest also goes back into your account. Some "experts" mention the fact that you are paying back this loan with after-tax money as a downside, but you would pay back any other loan with after-tax money as well too.

Employers that offer 401(k) loans have similar rules that must be consistent with IRS guidelines. I have listed ten things any daughter of mine should know about 401(k) loans, but you need check the exact terms and conditions of your employer's plan.

1. Typically, you can only borrow 50% of the account balance, up to $50,000.
2. The interest rate is usually the prime rate plus 1% or 2% (in 2012, the total interest rate from my company for a 401(k) loan was 3.25%).
3. There is normally an application fee of about $50 and possibly other fees.

4. You may be able to have more than one loan at the same time.
5. The loan is not reported to the credit reporting agencies.
6. It takes about 5 days to get the funds from the loan, via check or direct deposit into your bank account.
7. You usually have up to 5 years to pay back the loan (longer if it's for a primary residence).
8. Most plans allow you to pay back the loan early without penalty.
9. You can still contribute to your 401(k) while you are paying back the loan.
10. If you leave the company, the loan is payable in full within 60 days, or it will be treated as a withdrawal (which requires you to pay tax and a 10% penalty).

The biggest downside to taking a 401(k) loan is that you are interrupting your long-term savings. If you borrow from your account again and again, you are defeating the purpose of the account.

This is your money, but I would use the 401(k) loan only as a last resort or on rare occasions. If you are disciplined and strategic about it, a 401(k) loan can be great. So I'm saying, just proceed with caution.

Love,
Mom loaning some unpopular advice

*   *   *

Dear Amber,

Buying a home will likely be the largest purchase you will ever make. The financing for the home is called a *mortgage* and basically sets you up a on a monthly payment schedule (called amortization) to pay the home off over a specified term, most often fifteen or thirty years.

Mortgages can be very complicated instruments but are a necessary evil in order to borrow money to purchase a home. It could take months to sift through and learn everything there is about mortgages, so knowing that you would never do that, I am going to hit a few of the most important highlights for you in the letters that follow.

A couple of other great resources to learn about mortgages and home buying are www.homeloanlearningcenter.com, which is a website put out by the *Mortgage Bankers Association*, and www.bankrate.com, which is a great website for learning about mortgages and all things related to finances. The US Department of Housing and Urban Development also has a great home buying page at www.hud.gov/buying, which includes several quick reference brochures.

Love,
Mom lending some clarity

*   *   *

Dear Amber,

Home ownership used to be the American dream, but after the housing bubble burst in 2008, things changed drastically! There were a lot of people that purchased houses they could not afford, did not make any down payment, and did not have the credit to support the mortgages they received—all these things made possible by the banks and mortgage lenders.

This resulted in record foreclosures, short sales, and other distressed property because many homeowners could not pay their mortgages. On the flip side, it created a great buying opportunity for people with money and great credit looking to buy a home. Four years later in 2012, many of those opportunities still remain. Couple that with historically low mortgage rates (you can get a 30-year fixed loan for less than 4%), and you've got *the* best time to purchase a home in recent history.

With the low interest rates on mortgages, it also offered the opportunity for people to replace their existing loan with a new one, called a *refinance*. Even with the many rules surrounding a refinance that might eliminate some homeowners from qualifying, there have been special programs to help get them approved. Imagine going from paying 7.6% (the average 30-year fixed interest rate for the year you were born) to paying only 3.75% if you refinance now. Yes, interest rates are about half of what they were in 1995; take a look at the chart that follows.

Love,
Mom still believing in the American dream

Where Mortgage Rates have been over Amber's Lifetime

Average 30-year, Fixed-rate Mortgage

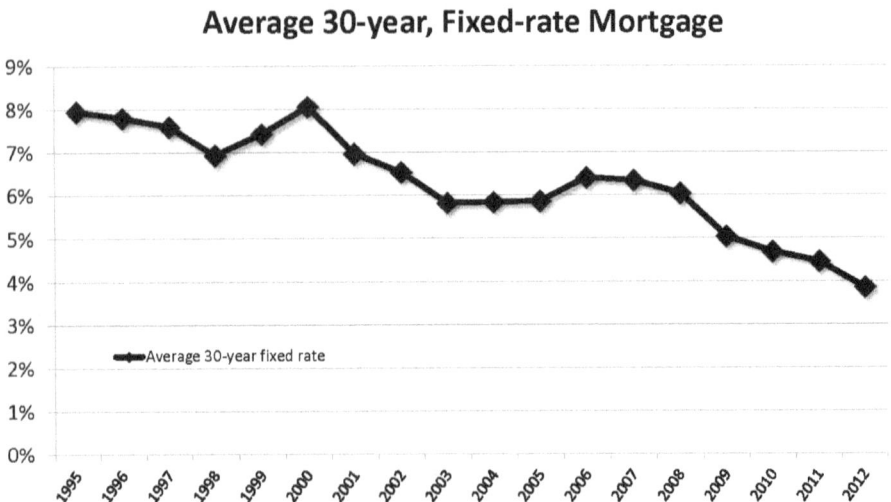

Source: Board of Governors of the Federal Reserve System, www.federalreserve.gov

*   *   *

Dear Amber,

You have many options for where you can get a loan, and probably my least favorite is a big national bank because that is likely where you will pay the highest rate, highest fees, and get the worst service. Be sure to shop and compare mortgages at credit unions, mortgage brokers, online banks, and small regional or local banks. The two primary things to look at as you shop and compare are *interest rate* and *closing costs*. Dig into these two things closely because there are a lot of variations with these two figures.

All mortgages are not created equal, so always make sure you read and understand the terms of what you think is the best mortgage for *you* (don't just listen to what the mortgage seller is telling you). The most common is a 30-year fixed, but you have 15-year fixed mortgages, adjustable-rate mortgages (ARM), interest-only mortgages, and who knows what new variations they will come up with in your lifetime.

Once you decide on the type of loan and your mortgage is set up, remember that your payment will also likely include the cost of property taxes and homeowners insurance and, possibly, private mortgage insurance (PMI) if you didn't put at least 20% down. The way the taxes and insurance gets paid is through what is called an *escrow* account. The escrow account holds the portion of your mortgage payment for the taxes and insurance (and PMI, if applicable) and sends the money directly to those companies for you.

Don't forget about the closing costs that will have to be paid on the new loan. Very often the closing costs can be paid to the buyer, by the seller of the home. These costs run about 3%-5% of the price of the home and are usually paid up front (a combination of fees and prepaid costs). Beware of the "no closing cost" loans because, most often, that just means the closing costs have been buried some where else, so you still have to pay them.

Love,
Mom simplifying a mortgage

*   *   *

Dear Amber,

One of the wisest ways to buy a home is to put enough of a down payment that will allow you to avoid private mortgage insurance (PMI), typically 20%. Get a fixed rate if you plan on staying in the home for more than five years. If you are going to stay in the house for less than five years, consider an adjustable rate mortgage ARM, you have a lower rate in the beginning and then the rate adjusts each year based on an index that is determined at the beginning of the loan. The terms of an ARM loan should be read very closely. With an ARM, you have just enough time to refinance the loan or sell the house.

When you are finally ready to close on your loan, the lender will put you in a small room and give you about an hour to sign stacks of paperwork, but you can ask to get this in advance so you can actually take your time to read and understand what you are signing. Your mortgage lender will probably be very surprised if you requested this because almost no one else does; most people just go along with whatever they are told, even when it doesn't make sense.

Love,
Mom mastering a complex instrument

*   *   *

CHAPTER 5

Saving Money

Saving money is how you begin your road to wealth. Paying your bills is very important, but always pay yourself too. Paying yourself is in the form of saving something every week, every month, every year for *you*. Save early and save often. Once you have accumulated a nice cushion of money (about six months worth of expenses), then you can start to invest.

Dear Amber,

I thought I would explain the difference between saving and investing. Saving is keeping your money safe and not spending it. Investing is putting your money at risk, usually with a chance of greater reward. When you are saving, it is typically kept in a financial institution (bank or credit union) where your principal is guaranteed and insured, and you get a small interest rate on that money. When you are investing, you put your money in things like stocks, bonds, mutual funds, or exchange traded funds (ETF). You can lose the money you put in or earn money on top of what you put in, depending on the performance of the investment. My rule is to save when you need the money short term like for an emergency or backup, and invest the money when it's for a longer-term need like retirement or your child's education.

Love,
Mom happy to save, happier to invest

*   *   *

Dear Amber,

I always want you to have fun and enjoy the money that you have worked so hard for. Well, I know you really fluff off a lot, but let's pretend that you actually work hard on something that I might not be aware of. The one small thing that I want you to do is always pay yourself first—maybe start with 10%. So let's do the math that you learned in school and you said you would never use in real life: If your weekly paycheck is only $80, then 10% would be $8. Put that $8 into a savings account every week for a rainy day (which I guarantee will come). If your paycheck is $1,000 a week, then 10% would be $100. When you get a raise in pay, increase your savings instead of increasing your spending. If you take these habits with you all your life, you'll be better, richer, and feel financially freer than anyone else around you. The huge advantage you have over me at a such a young age is *time*. The earlier you start, the more time you have for your money to grow; I wish I would have started earlier. For now, please just clean that stinky cat litter!

Love,
Mom with a marginal propensity to save

* * *

Dear Amber,

Once you get the hang of saving money, try to next get to at least $1,000 for your "get out of trouble" fund, since trouble seems to follow you whenever I'm not around. Like the time you rear-ended another car at a red light because you were texting and driving after you only had your license for a few months. Well, you get the point; $1,000 will help you pay for most unexpected situations.

Once you have reached your $1,000, you should work to save about 3-6 months' worth of expenses. This will keep you from freaking out if you lose your job (because you will still be able to pay your bills) or minimize the stress level if you have to get a major repair to your car (hopefully not from another accident!).

Now that you have done a great job with saving some cash to ease your mind a little, you are ready to invest.

Love,
Mom advocating the relief of stress and anxiety

* * *

Dear Amber,

Most people are just a paycheck away from being broke; you and I know plenty of them. Living this way is quite miserable, so I want to make sure that you, my dear, are never in that place because you are way too smart to live paycheck to paycheck. So as you start saving just the 10% or so of each paycheck you get, you will begin to accumulate an emergency fund that will always give you something to fall back on and priceless peace of mind. Sure, some people just have the natural inclination to save (and I'm convinced you do), but if you don't have that savings gene, then marry it!

Love,
Mom against living paycheck to paycheck

*   *   *

Dear Amber,

When you start to save, think of it as paying yourself first. You have to pay your bills, pay for gas, pay for rent, pay for buying new clothes, and many other things that gobble up your paycheck. Paying for these things is very important, but what is even more important is paying yourself—*first.* That means before your money goes to anything else, set aside something to put into your savings account every time you get paid.

The absolutely easiest way to make sure that you pay yourself first is make it automatic. You can have a weekly transfer from your checking account to your savings account. This is something you don't have to think about, and since that money is not in your hands, you won't even have the temptation of spending it on something worth a lot less than your peace of mind.

Love,
Mom paying herself first

*   *   *

Dear Amber,

Always set aside a nest egg for yourself. Even after you are married. Even after you have kids. Always have a little for yourself. If you ask me or probably anyone else for money, we are going to ask a lot of questions and get all in your business like you hate. So by setting aside money for yourself, you are really telling me to mind my own business (not that I will always listen). Rainy days will always come.

Love,
Mom supporting self-reliance

*   *   *

Dear Amber,

You've asked me, "When I first start saving, where is the best place to put my money?" Well, the short answer is head to the web and find an online bank. They typically pay much better interest rates than the big national banks because online banks don't have the overhead expenses of maintaining local branches (a building, staffing, etc.). Online banks also usually have much lower fees and better benefits (I've been gladly using the same online bank, E*TRADE, for the last 15 years).

When you were taking karate classes in the fifth grade, interest rates on savings accounts were over 5% at many online banks; but now that you are a varsity cheerleader in high school, you are lucky to get a 1% interest rate on your savings. In fact, in 2012, the highest rate I found was at TIAA Direct (www.tiaadirect.com) with a 1.24% interest rate for their high-yield savings account. Oh, and this account had no monthly fee and no minimum balance required.

Take a look at how interest rates have changed over your lifetime:

Where Savings Interest Rates have been over Amber's Lifetime

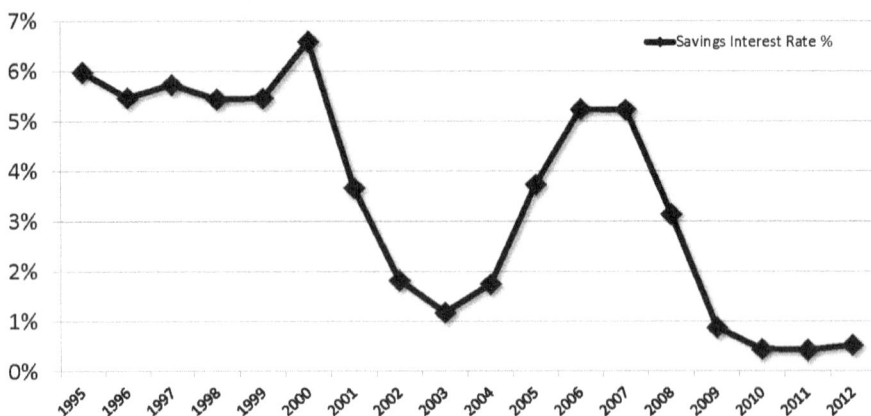

Source: Board of Governors of the Federal Reserve System, www.federalreserve.gov

Regardless of the fluctuations in interest rates, you will often get a better rate online, and some banks will even offer a bonus to open an account. There are many websites that will list banks with the highest interest rates like www.bankrate.com, www.bankaholic.com, and www.savingsaccounts.com, or just go to Google or Yahoo! and search for top interest rates for savings.

Just make sure that any bank you deal with is *FDIC* insured (or *NCUA* insured if it's a credit union), which means, if the institution goes bust, you don't lose all the money you have with them. You can verify this information about your bank at www.fdic.gov or credit union at www.ncua.gov. The *Bank of Mom* is not FDIC insured.

Love,
Mom desperately seeking higher rates

*   *   *

Dear Amber,

You have asked me why I have collected so many $2 bills over the years. I know it is a little eccentric (a nice word for crazy) that I have saved over 1,800 $2 bills, worth over $3,600 in total, but the answer is simple: if they were $1 bills, I would have spent them all by now.

It was just another way for me to save rather than spend. Every time I went to a bank, I would ask the teller for $2 bills. After over 20 years of doing that, it just added up. One day, I'll pass this $2 bill collection on to you (which I am sure you will spend on worthless crap), but hopefully you will appreciate the lesson that saving even the smallest amount adds up.

Love,
Mom convinced $2 bills are better than ones

*   *   *

CHAPTER 6

Investing Money

Once you have saved enough money to serve as an emergency fund in case you ever need the cash (about six months worth of expenses), you should start investing. When you are investing, you are putting your money at risk, but with the potential of great reward. The reward is a return on your money that has proven to be a great deal better over time. Investing your money wisely is your path to wealth. If you invest early and invest often, you will see your money grow.

Dear Amber,

Did you know that it takes just $50 a week for you to become a millionaire? Assuming a 9% annual rate of return by investing in the stock market, you would have a million dollars over a 40-year period. No joke! Pretty amazing, huh? If you and your friends want to take this challenge, I will give you the first $50 to get started after you graduate high school.

Take a look at the chart that shows three different ways you can easily get to $1 million by investing regularly over time. Also, feel free to try whatever scenario you want by using an online calculator, like the one you can find at www.dinkytown.com or www.bankrate.com.

Love,
Mom turning $50 tricks

3 Easy ways to get to $1 million

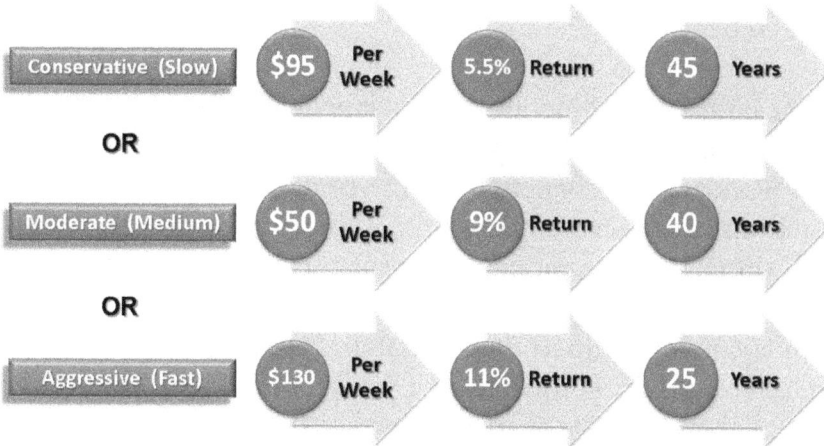

| Conservative (Slow) | $95 Per Week | 5.5% Return | 45 Years |

OR

| Moderate (Medium) | $50 Per Week | 9% Return | 40 Years |

OR

| Aggressive (Fast) | $130 Per Week | 11% Return | 25 Years |

= $1,000,000

* * *

Dear Amber,

Please remember that most financial professionals don't know much more than you do about money. Most of them are just financial salespeople that sell you what they make the highest commission on. Not that anything is wrong with salespeople (because your mom is one), but I just want my baby to know when a slick financial guy comes to you *guaranteeing* 10% returns consistently, every single year, he's probably full of—it. Google *Bernie Madoff.*

Now let me not discredit every financial professional out there. There are some reputable ones that are dedicated to putting the needs of their clients first. You just have to do your research and feel comfortable with the person that you choose to manage your money. The website www.finra.gov has lots of helpful information on this.

Love,
Mom entering the full realm of paranoia

* * *

Dear Amber,

The largest pot of money that most people will ever have in their lifetime is their employer-sponsored retirement plan, like a 401(k). It has wonderful tax benefits and the beauty of regular, automatic deductions from every paycheck. Typically, companies offer a match on part of the money you contribute to your 401(k)—yes, free money!

Today, many employers will match dollar for dollar up to 3% of what you put in. For instance, if you make $30,000 per year and you contribute just 3% of that to your 401(k), that would be $900 per year. With your dollar for dollar company match, that amount would double to *$1,800*! If you took advantage of this from the time you started your career at age 22, contributed this $900 per year, plus got a company match of $900, you would have over $1 million by the time you retire at age 65 (assuming about a 9%

return). This is just another easy way to get to being a millionaire with the help of your company.

So can you do me a favor? Never pass up free money like this!

Love,
Mom that loves a good match

Getting to an easy Million with your 401(k)

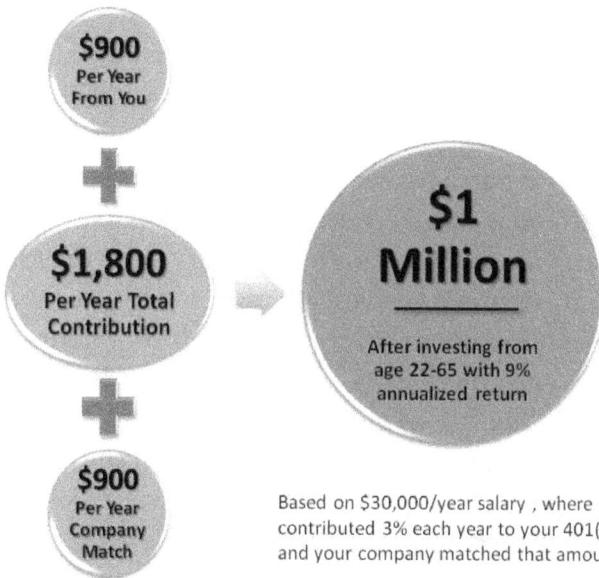

$900
Per Year
From You

+

$1,800
Per Year Total
Contribution

+

$900
Per Year
Company
Match

$1 Million
_____
After investing from
age 22-65 with 9%
annualized return

Based on $30,000/year salary , where you contributed 3% each year to your 401(k)--$900, and your company matched that amount.

* * *

Dear Amber,

With regards to social security for your retirement—there won't be any. As a matter of fact, there will hardly be any left when I retire. Lucky for you, I have planned so that you won't have the burden of taking care of me in my old age. I hope you give the same gift to your children.

Love,
A-victim-of-the-federal-deficit Mom

*　　*　　*

Dear Amber,

I know that you will never take the time to read and understand the IRS rules on Roth IRAs even if I gave you this link: http://www.irs.gov/pub/irs-pdf/p590.pdf and asked you to just click on it to instantly get there. So let me help you decipher all the confusing and conflicting information about a very simple account that is hugely beneficial to most people:

- You pay regular taxes on the money you contribute to a Roth IRA, but you can take out those same *contributions* anytime you want and pay *no tax* and *no penalties—ever* (my favorite part about this account). So you can use that money (only the contributions) for a down payment on a house or other mom-approved financial moves with no tax or penalties. When it comes to the *earnings* on your contributions, those may be subject to taxes and penalties if you take them out before the age of eligibility.
- If you listened to anything else I taught you about investments, you will earn money on top of your contributions. The money that you earn does have penalties and taxes if you take it out before you are old like me (I know you think I'm over 60, but I'm not) or have the account for less than 5 years, so don't do it.
- The reward for saving early using a Roth IRA is that the tax bracket you are in at age 22 is likely to be a lot lower than when you are age 50. For example, if you save $10,000 while you are in your 20s, you may only pay $800 in taxes on that; but at age 50 (when you are probably earning more and in a higher tax bracket), you would have to pay about $2,000 on that same $10,000. If you have this money in a Roth IRA, you won't pay any taxes on it if you withdraw the contributions at age 50 because you already paid the taxes up front at a much lower rate.

- Roth accounts are very easy to open online, and you can contribute up to $5,000 per year if you make less than $110,000 per year (as of 2012). If you make more than that, well then, that means that you finished college and chose a career that is paying you what you are worth (that's my girl). It's puzzling to me why the government limits your saving on this account when I always told you how important it is to save. Just don't let that discourage you, there is always another way. Come talk to mom and we'll figure it out.

Love,
Mom performing her fiduciary duty

*   *   *

Dear Amber,

When you decide to start saving for your child's education, the best way to do that is a 529 plan or Coverdell Educational Savings Account (ESA).

A 529 plan is an education savings plan sponsored by a state. The contribution limits are much more generous than with the Coverdell ESA, with most states allowing about $300,000 total. Just like the Coverdell ESA, you have to pay taxes on the contributions up front, but when you take the money out for qualified college expenses, you don't have to pay any taxes on the contributions or the growth. With these accounts, you do need to be careful about fees. You can find the best-rated 529 plans and how to open one at www.savingforcollege.com or www.clarkhoward.com.

The Coverdell ESA is not as widely used as the 529 plan but does not require sponsorship from a state. It limits your contributions to $2,000 per year (in 2012), and there are some changes coming in 2013 that may reduce that even further. You can open an account with any of the online brokers and invest in just about anything like stocks, bonds, mutual funds, exchange traded funds (ETF), etc. You do have to pay taxes on the contributions, but when you are ready to take money out for qualified college expenses, you don't have to pay any taxes. You can learn more about the Coverdell ESA at www.savingforcollege.com.

Love,
Mom that knows the best things in life aren't always free

*   *   *

Dear Amber,

When you are ready to open your own investment account, I recommend starting online. Your generation definitely has the easy button on this one.

Most of the major discount brokers offer online account set up and walk you through each step. They also may offer a bonus for opening a new account with them, like cash in your account or free trades for the first couple of months. So they hold your hand and give you free money. Hmmm . . . that sounds a lot like Mom, doesn't it?

Here are a few more things I want you to know about online brokers:

- Most of them charge $4-$10 to buy or sell a stock.
- It will only take about $50 to get started.
- Most of them have a group of exchange traded funds (ETFs) and mutual funds available that have no transaction fee.
- Every broker will have some type of online tools to help you analyze stocks and other investments.
- You can find reviews and ratings of brokers at www. stockbrokers.com or www.brokerage-review.com.

Love,
Mom giving stamp of approval to online brokers

*   *   *

Dear Amber,

I wanted to convey to you how much your money grows by investing in the stock market. It can be risky, but over time, this is the best place to have your money to get the highest returns. If you took the S&P 500 (one of the most commonly used benchmarks for the overall US stock market), it has had an average return of about 10% over your lifetime. And the best year during that period was the year you were born! Take a look at the following chart:

Performance of Stocks over Amber's Lifetime

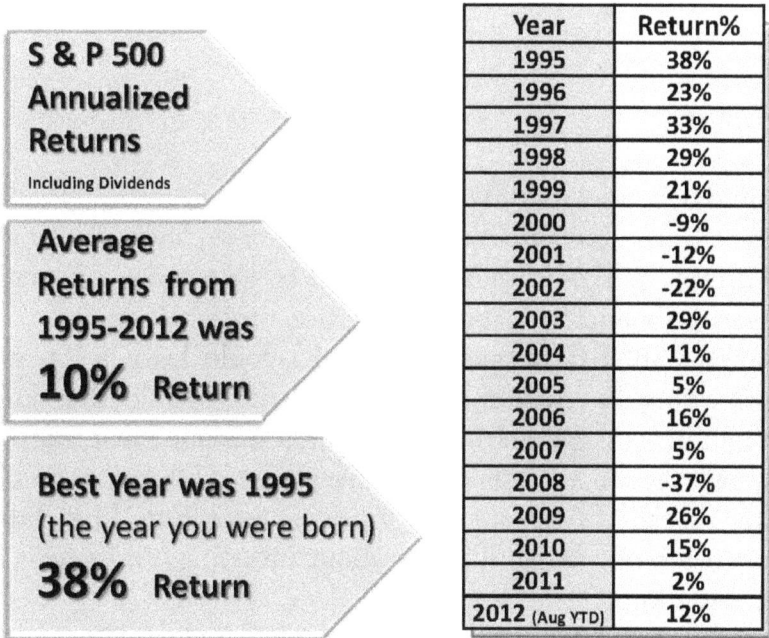

S & P 500
Annualized
Returns
Including Dividends

Average
Returns from
1995-2012 was
10% Return

Best Year was 1995
(the year you were born)
38% Return

Year	Return%
1995	38%
1996	23%
1997	33%
1998	29%
1999	21%
2000	-9%
2001	-12%
2002	-22%
2003	29%
2004	11%
2005	5%
2006	16%
2007	5%
2008	-37%
2009	26%
2010	15%
2011	2%
2012 (Aug YTD)	12%

Source: S&P, www.standardandpoors.com

You don't have to use individual stocks to get to these kinds of returns. Instead, you can invest in a basket of stocks, which is usually in the form of an ETF or mutual fund. These funds will help you spread your risk, and you won't have all your eggs in one basket.

There are many financial websites that do a great job of helping you better understand this and the other basics of investing. One of my favorite is Clark Howard's Investment Guide at www.clarkhoward.com. Clark Howard is the consumer advocate and money expert that I consider to be my best teacher. He hosts a well-respected radio show and has published a number of resources to help teach and empower consumers when it comes to all kinds of money matters. Most of the online brokers will have an education section that is usually very helpful as well.

Love,
Mom praising the time value of money

*   *   *

Dear Amber,

I would be remiss if I did not mention the greatest thing that has helped me learn about investing, the *Cincinnati Model Investment Club* (CinMIC). This club is an affiliate of *BetterInvesting*, which is a national non-profit investor education organization.

I joined CinMIC because I figured I could learn a lot more about investing by surrounding myself with people that know more about investing than me. Turns out, it has done just that, and I would rely on the analysis of this investment club much quicker than any so-called "expert" on a business program. The club is all about teaching people like me about investing, and I love the collective wisdom.

BetterInvesting has four principles for successful long-term investing, which I think are keys to anyone wanting to get serious about investing:

- Invest regularly
- Reinvest all earnings
- Invest in growth companies and growth funds
- Diversify to reduce risk

When you have the inclination to learn more about investing, check out www.betterinvesting.org.

Love,
Mom that's a better investor today than she was yesterday

*   *   *

CHAPTER 7

Money and Taxes

There is a saying that the two sure things in life are death and taxes. It's the truth. Just about everything you do has a tax implication. You buy something, you have to pay taxes; you get a job, you have to pay taxes; you make money off your investments, you have to pay taxes. Taxes will become more important as you go through life and accumulate wealth.

Dear Amber,

As you start out in the working world, you may not be making much money at first—perhaps while you are paying your own way through college? Well, there is a little-known tax credit just for you and other low-income people who save for retirement. If you contribute to a retirement account such as an IRA or 401(k) and you make less than $28,250 a year (in 2011), you may be able to claim the saver's credit. This credit is worth up to $1,000 for you. Never turn down free money, especially from the government, to whom you will be giving much of your hard-earned money anyway.

Ooops, news flash. Just like the government, there are some restrictions to this benefit that will exclude any person born after 1993 and full-time students. I guess that would leave you out, but please pass this on to your friends that might actually meet the restrictive criteria.

Love,
Mom urging the government to cast a wider net

*   *   *

Dear Amber,

If you look closely at your paycheck, you will notice that taxes are automatically withheld from your pay, complements of the government. You don't have a choice of whether you want to pay these because employers are required to withhold these taxes for their employees. Here are the main types of taxes that are withheld from your paycheck:

Types of Payroll Taxes

Federal	State	SS/Medicare (FICA)
• Collected by IRS to fund the country's expenses	• Collected by your state to fund the expenses of the state	• Federal program that provides income and health insurance for the elderly and disabled

Love,
Duly-taxed Mom

*   *   *

Dear Amber,

Since you have started working, you will need to file your income tax returns every year. These days, that is mostly done electronically. As simple as yours are just starting out, you should be able to file your federal taxes for free. You can go to the Internal Revenue Service website (www.irs.gov/freefile), and they will provide you with a list of where you can file for free. I know that Turbo Tax is just one of the programs that allow you to electronically file a 1040EZ for free (the very simple tax form, taking the standard deduction). Most states also offer free filings of your income tax return; just go to your state's tax website.

Love,
Mom supporting free filing

*   *   *

Dear Amber,

Even when your taxes become a little more complicated, I would recommend that you stick with Turbo Tax because it is very easy to use and guides you step by step on what to do and what information to enter. I learned a lot doing Turbo Tax and feel that I can do a much better job than some quickie tax preparation geek that just went through a two-week class.

I used one of these places once and figured they knew what they were doing. I ended up paying about $300 to have my taxes done, only to find out later that he made some big mistakes that cost me. The main thing was that he made me take the standard deduction (aka the easy deduction), when he should have asked me what other deductions I had so that I could itemize my deductions (listing everything out and taking a little longer) and possibly get more money back. The fact that I owned a home and could deduct my taxes and interest on that really made a difference (I didn't know that at the time). This annoyed me for several years, so I finally researched how I could fix this and found out a way for me to amend my taxes for that year and reverse the mistake this idiot made. I got back about $600, plus interest from the IRS. I felt better after that.

Love,
Do-it-yourself Mom

*   *   *

CHAPTER 8

Things Money Can't Buy

All the wisdom I have gained and shared with you in my letters about money means a lot, but not everything. Yes, money makes the world go around, but I also learned that there are some things that money can't buy. These things mold and shape who we are, but you could never put a price tag on them. Be sure to pay close attention to these next few letters, and remember that all money decisions, no matter how big or small, have an emotional motivator driving them.

Dear Amber,

You got your driver's license today, and I know this means the world to you. I am happy too and knew you would pass your road test with flying colors. I just looked at a picture of you that I keep at the office. You were about three years old and gave me the biggest smile. Even though you are many years older and several feet taller now, I can't help but think of my little three-year-old peeking over the steering wheel. I wish I could buy back the time with my three-year-old.

Love,
Sentimental Mom

*   *   *

Dear Amber,

When it comes to money (or just about anything else), you learn more by asking questions than trying to give all the answers. When you have a money question, I guarantee that you'll have many people trying to give you the answers but really don't know any more than you. You'll know if you should listen to them or not by asking questions like "How did you learn about that?" "Did that work for you?" "Can you give me more details?" Someone that you don't want to listen to will probably have these answers to those questions: "My cousin." "Well, I haven't tried it yet." "Nope, I just know it's right. I would ask my cousin, but he is in jail right now, so I can't."

Love,
Inquisitive Mom

*   *   *

Dear Amber,

At every stage of your life, you should always find room to give back. There are so many people in need and are less fortunate than you. Things you take for granted like having a good meal every day, a closet full of clothes and good health, may be a luxury for some people. You can give money, but don't forget how valuable it is to also share your time, talents, and expertise with others.

I love this quote from my favorite poet, Maya Angelou: "I've learned that you shouldn't go through life with a catcher's mitt on both hands; you need to be able to throw something back."

There are thousands of charities dedicated to many different causes in the US and abroad that you can contribute to, or just start your own. Find your cause and decide how you want to help. It will warm your heart, balance your life, and make you feel wealthier every day.

Love,
Mom urging you to throw something back

*   *   *

Dear Amber,

I know this is going to be hard for you to swallow, but I want to let you know that it is okay to *not* know everything. As a matter of fact, it's a good thing because if you knew everything, you would never have the opportunity to learn something new. I actually have a better day anytime I can learn something new, so my new five favorite words are "I learned something new today."

I remember when you were a little girl; you were always so curious and asked so many questions. You don't ask me very many questions anymore; I miss that. Instead, you try to give me all the answers. I know that one day you will no doubt be much smarter than me, but today you are not. So can we both just *learn something new today"?*

Love,
Mom happy she learned something new today

*　*　*

Dear Amber,

Money can buy you an education, but it can't buy you knowledge—you have to get that from your desire and passion to learn. I had to work my way through college because it wasn't free, and I didn't have the luxury of someone else paying for it.

Many years later—long after I graduated from college, long after my first few moves, and long after my first few jobs—I realized that I learned more from working while I was going to school than what my professors taught me in the classroom. I learned how to manage my money and make every dollar count. I figured out many ways to help me raise my tuition money, like scholarships, grants, tuition assistance from work, and internships.

I'm sure you know that I really suck at sports, so when my college freshman gym teacher asked me to be on the school's cross-country team, I told him he was crazy, and I was not very athletic at all. I further let him know that the only reason I was even taking his gym class in the first place was because I heard it was an easy A. Then, that magical word came out of his mouth—*scholarship.* So I gladly joined the team and enjoyed that scholarship money for the next three years. It didn't cover all my college expenses, but it sure was nice to have that help!

Love,
Self-funded Mom

*　*　*

Dear Amber,

Soon after you have started working, you will surely be asked by one of our family members to borrow money. So that you can hopefully avoid being in that uncomfortable position, which I was many times, I wanted to pass on what I think is the best way to handle it.

Make sure they know that you don't have a pile of money just sitting around to loan out, but you have a few dollars (always less than $20) that you are happy to give them. Let them know that they can pay you back if they want, but they don't have to. This gives them an opening to show if they have any real interest in doing the right thing and giving you the money back or at least return some type of in-kind gesture (like washing your car, babysitting, etc.)

Anyone that really appreciates what you have given them will always find a way to thank you. If they don't, then they have taken you for granted, and you should think twice about giving them money again. Usually, if you give them money more than once, they will ask many times after that, and before you know, you've created a leach. This is kind of how I felt shortly after you became a teenager, and you thought I was the *bank of motherly love.*

Love,
Giving (not loaning) Mom

* * *

Dear Amber,

I want you to be aware of your rights as a consumer to complain. If you have issues that are not resolved to your satisfaction with a company you are doing business with, there are many agencies where you can file an official complaint, like the Better Business Bureau (www.bbb.org) and your state's attorney general's office (www.naag.org). There is even a very special agency specifically designed to address consumer complaints of banks and other financial institutions called the *Consumer Financial Protection Bureau* (CFPB) (www.consumerfinance.gov/complaint).

You can also try using unofficial resources like consumer complaint or business rating websites, like Yelp (www.yelp.com). If you are really bold (and I know you are), post a video on YouTube (www.youtube.com). If the video is compelling enough, I'll bet your issue will get resolved real quick.

Use these resources, official and unofficial, to exercise your rights and stand up and fight when you've been mistreated.

Love,
Mom raising a complainer

*   *   *

Dear Amber,

Sometimes you do deserve a free lunch, like on your birthday. But Mom's not paying for it. There are a ton of restaurants that offer a free meal or dessert on your birthday. Guess what the website is? Good guess, www.freebirthday.com.

Love,
Mom wishing you a happy birthday

*   *   *

Dear Amber,

History starts today, with money and everything else. Don't let bad decisions in the past discourage you from making things better in the future. Great things are accomplished over time, but they all began on just one day. So you, my daughter, start with today; and before you know it, you will have changed your history. My most important history started the day you were born.

Love,
Mom with a history

*   *   *

Dear Amber,

I'm not going to tell you who to vote for when it comes to political candidates because I am not very involved in that circus. Sorry to characterize it like that, but if you google *Washington three ring circus debt ceiling*, you'll see what I mean. The way politicians in Washington argue back and forth without ever really getting anything done reminds me of when you were in first grade and got in a fight with the boy in your class over crayons. Instead of boys and girls, it's Republicans and Democrats that are constantly bickering, don't play fair and never see the other kid's side.

Know that your money problems will not get solved by two sides that are always at odds with each other. Also, reminiscent of your first grade behavior is the budgeting philosophy of the government: they think there is a magical ATM somewhere spouting money and have no regard for who really is paying for things. You need to make your financial decisions independent of what the politicians do or who's in running the country.

Love,
Politically incorrect Mom

*   *   *

Dear Amber,

Just another quick letter about politics. It has become very hard to really research the candidates that are running for office. They all sound great while they are campaigning, but later you realize they can't deliver on what they promised. No matter how many questions are asked, they never seem to give a straight answer. So how do you decide? I don't know, but I am convinced that the politicians all read from the same books: "101 Ways to Squirm Out of Any Question" and "How to Backpedal While Looking Like You Are Moving Ahead."

Love,
Cynical Mom

*   *   *

Dear Amber,

So you see that I am not a fan of politics, but I still vote. My primary reason is that many years ago, women and blacks were not allowed to vote. So when I exercise that right, it is in the name of those before me that could not.

Love,
Mom voting for something bigger than herself

*   *   *

Dear Amber,

Over the years of watching you become an adult, as well as many of my friends and family, I think I have uncovered a scientific theory of something called the parent appreciation factor. I believe that I have come up with the trend of how a child's appreciation of their parents changes with their age. Quite interesting, it's kind of like a V shape as you go through life from infancy to old age. I know how visual you are, so to help illustrate this trend line, I have developed a graph. The parent appreciation factor is on a scale from 0 to 100, where 100 is the best score (meaning you appreciate your parents a lot), and 0 is the worst (meaning you don't appreciate your parents at all—they suck). I also made some comments that you likely had at each stage of your life for each score.

Legend:

100 = I appreciate my parents a lot
0 = I don't appreciate my parents at all (they suck)

Parent Appreciation Factor

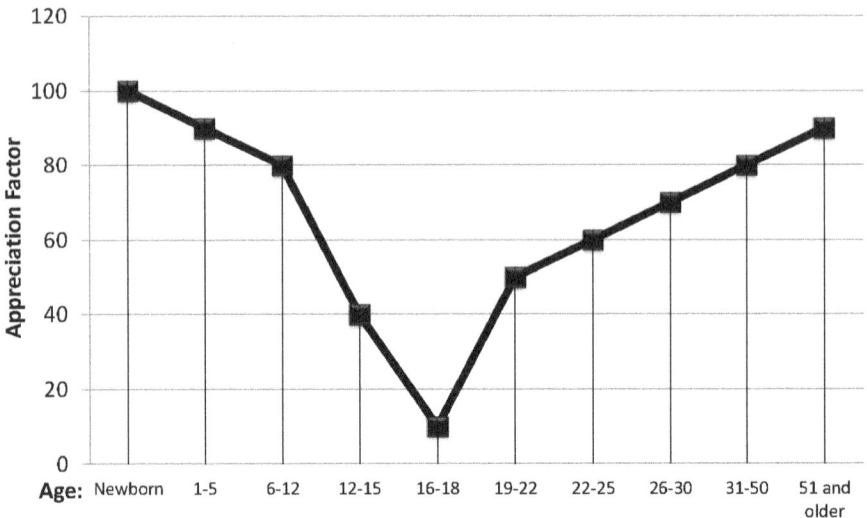

Amber's Appreciation of Mom

AGE	PARENT APPRECIATION FACTOR	LINE OF THINKING
Newborn	100	Mom brought me in this world, she is everything to me
1-5	90	Mom is bigger than life and takes care of all my needs
6-12	80	Mom is not letting me be independent, but I can do things for myself now. Leave me alone.
12-15	40	Mom is starting to annoy me big time and won't let me be my own person : (
16-18	10	Mom is ruining my life and I secretly wish she would jump off a cliff
19-22	50	Mom's not so bad, I at least have to keep her around to pay for my college and get a free ride for just a little bit longer
22-25	60	Oh crap, do I really have to take care of myself now? Maybe mom isn't so bad, I'll keep pretending she matters
26-30	70	I'm married with kids. Now I understand what my mom was trying to teach me and how much she loves me
31-50	80	I have the ultimate appreciation for my mom now because it was her that always taught me to work smart, dream big and achieve greatness in everything I do
51 and older	90	Mom is no longer around, but her wise words, strong spirit and life lessons will always be with me

Love,
Occasionally unappreciated Mom

*   *   *

Dear Amber,

I have learned a great deal about money over the years, but not without the help of people much smarter than me. So I wanted to take a moment to share with you just a few of the resources that have taught me the most:

Clark Howard Show (www.clarkhoward.com)
> My absolute favorite consumer advocate and money expert to listen to on the radio, podcasts, and TV.

Suze Orman Show (www.suzeorman.com)
> My favorite personal finance expert who gives advice via TV, magazines, books, podcasts, and website.

CNBC (www.cnbc.com)
> My favorite TV channel to watch the markets throughout the day, especially Squawk Box and Mad Money.

Market Place Money Podcast (www.marketplace.org)
> One of my favorite podcasts that covers money topics with reputable guests I always learn from.

Yahoo! Finance (www.finance.yahoo.com)
> My favorite website to watch the stock market, research stocks, maintain all my stock portfolios, looking at daily mortgage rates, read money articles, and find other financial information.

Dinkytown (www.dinkytown.net)
> Every financial calculator you'd ever need (for credit cards, savings, mortgage, etc.).

Talk Credit Radio with Gerri Detweiler (www.gerridetweiler.com)
> I love listening to this podcast and appreciate the expertise and knowledge shared by the host and guests

Money Guy Podcast (www.money-guy.com)
> This podcast is done by an investment professional that I think is very smart and honest. He covers a variety of topics on money and investing.

Money Girl: Quick & Dirty Tips (www.quickanddirtytips.com)
> The podcasts and articles do a great job of explaining complex personal finance issues in a short and concise manner.

FINRA Education Foundation (www.finrafoundation.org)
> Nonprofit arm of the agency that regulates the financial and securities industry.

Investopedia (www.investopedia.com)
> A well-organized encyclopedia and dictionary for investing and other financial topics.

Maxed Out (http://topdocumentaryfilms.com/maxed-out/)
>A shocking documentary about escalating consumer debt that pulls back the curtain on big banks and their shameful part in America's debt crisis. You can watch it for free at this website.

Love,
Mom learning from the experts

*   *   *

Dear Amber,

Here is my advice on how you should prioritize your money issues once you are working and on your own:

1. Save a small part of what you earn in an account that you can get to quickly in an emergency.
2. If your employer offers a match for your 401(k) account, contribute at least the amount they will match (remember, don't give up free money!).
3. Start making above the minimum payments on high interest debts, beginning with the highest to the lowest.
4. Open a Roth IRA as soon as all your high interest debt is paid off. It is okay to still have lower interest, longer term loans like a mortgage, student loan, or car loan. The Roth IRA will double as an emergency fund and future long-term savings.
5. Set your short-term savings goals, like the down payment on a house or something smart like that. Make this automatic and let this short-term account only be a portion of what you are saving. The other portion should be for long-term savings like retirement.
6. Max out your annual Roth IRA ($5,000 in 2012). You could consider using your contributions only to help with

a down payment on a house, but be careful about dipping into this account.

7. Max out your annual 401(k) ($17,000 in 2012).

If you still have money left over, please celebrate and reward yourself because most people never make it beyond paying off their debt (what a shame). But you, my dear, I know will master this quickly and enjoy all the rewards that follow wise planning and forethought in managing your money (oh, and having a great mom to teach you too).

Love,
Mom with a balanced budget

*   *   *

Dear Amber,

You have many more options to fund your college education than I have to fund my retirement. Now, I fully intend to help with your college education, and the best way I can do that is by helping you to help yourself. I don't want you to fall into the spoiled kid's zone, which shamefully supports the over privileged and excessively served. I know you don't want to be a member of that club. Take a look at all the ways a student has to pay for college against only a few ways a parent has to pay for their retirement. So parents should not feel guilty by putting their retirement first and saving for college second; it's just what makes sense.

Money available to help pay for college:

- Part-time/Full-time job
- Grants
- Scholarships
- Internships

- Fellowships
- Work study
- GI Bill
- Military tuitions assistance programs
- Tuition reimbursement from employer
- Student loans

Money available to help pay for retirement:

- Social security (disappearing)
- Pension (unheard of these days)
- Retirement account (this is the only thing I can depend on because I fund that myself)

Love,
Mom no longer feeling guilty

*   *   *

CLOSING LETTER

Dear Amber,

I am giving you three copies of this book: one for you to keep, one for you to give to your daughter, and one to give to your granddaughter. My hope is that by then, the generational chain of bad money decisions will have been forever broken.

Love,
Mom with a succession plan

*   *   *

Directory of Letters

WEBSITES REFERENCED

Consumer Education
  www.clarkhoward.com
  www.suzeorman.com
  www.saveandinvest.org
  www.consumerfinance.gov
  www.smartbalancetransfers.com
  www.marketplace.org
  www.bbb.org
  www.federalreserveeducation.org
  www.pathwaytofinancialsuccess.org

Investing/Investor Education
  www.finrafoundation.org
  www.betterinvesting.org
  www.saveandinvest.org
  www.investopedia.org
  www.stockbrokers.com
  www.yahoofinance.com

www.cnbc.com
www.money-guy.com
www.standardandpoors.com
www.brokerage-review.com

Banking/Credit Card Services
www.bankrate.com
www.creditcards.com
www.bankaholic.com
www.savingsaccounts.com
www.smartbalancetransfers.com
www.penfed.org
www.discover.com
www.capitalone.com
www.tiaadirect.com

Credit Reports and Scores
www.annualcreditreport.com
www.saveandinvest.org/military
www.experian.com
www.gerridetweiler.com
www.transunion.com
www.equifax.com
www.myfico.com
www.quizzle.com
www.creditkarma.com

College
www.finaid.org
www.studentloans.gov
www.savingforcollege.com
www.fastweb.com
www.ibrinfo.org
www.studentloanborrowerassistance.org
www.projectonstudentdebt.org

Mortgages
    www.homeloanlearningcenter.com
    www.mortgagebankers.org
    www.bankrate.com
    www.hud.gov
    www.hud.gov/buying/booklet.pdf

Vehicles
    www.ase.org
    www.aaa.org
    www.edmunds.com
    www.kbb.com
    www.nada.com
    www.cars.com
    www.autotrader.com
    www.carsforsale.com

Government
    www.benefits.gov
    www.bls.gov
    www.consumerfinance.gov
    www.irs.gov
    www.hud.gov
    www.fdic.gov
    www.federalreserve.gov
    www.ncua.gov
    www.safecar.gov
    www.studentloans.gov

Others
    www.military.com
    www.missingmoney.com
    www.truecostofhealthcare.com
    www.gasbuddy.com
    www.freebirthday.com
    www.youtube.com
    www.yelp.com

Index

D

E

H

I

J

K

L

law, federal, 56, 79
loan
  against a vehicle, 42
  agreement, 32
  ARM, 88
  car, 32, 42, 60, 64
  "no closing cost," 87
  federal government, 73
  in general, 31–32, 60, 77, 80–82, 85–86
  interest-free, 53
  payday, 37, 77
  servicer, 73
  student, 60, 72–73, 121, 123
  where to get, 87

M

Mad Money, 120
Madoff, Bernie, 98
Market Place Money Podcast, 120
Maxed Out, 121
medicine, 38–41, 73
military, 58, 79, 81, 131–32
million, 52, 97–99
Missing Money, 25, 132
money
  advice about, 10, 15
  basics about, 10
  earning, 19, 21–22, 24
  investing, 10, 96
  managing, 15, 98
  for one's self, 29, 90
  in a plan account, 40

fixed, 88
hike, 42
refinance, 80, 86, 88
refund, 45
Republicans, 116
retail, 28
retirement, 83, 90, 99, 107, 121–23
Roth IRA (Individual Retirement Arrangement), 100, 107, 121

S

salesperson, 33, 35
savings, 39, 84, 92–94, 121
scams, 38, 76
scholarship, 113
SCRA (Servicemembers Civil Relief Act), 79
service industry, 23
sites
  car valuation, 34–35
  certified mechanic, 33
  estimate or simulations, 58
  government benefits, 26
  online shopping for cars at, 35
Smart Balance Transfers, 50
soapbox, 10
social security, 99, 123
S&P 500, *103*
Squawk Box, 120
stocks, 25, 28, 90, 97, 101–3, 120
strategies, priority, 74
Suze Orman Show, 120

T

Talk Credit Radio, 120
taxes, 40, 46, 76, 100–101, 106–9

www.ingramcontent.com/pod-product-compliance
Lightning Source LLC
Chambersburg PA
CBHW031406180326
41458CB00043B/6626/J